ONLY SA
WORD

365 Days Of Reflection On The Word Of God

FR. EMMANUEL GUKENA OKAMI

ISBN: 979-856-751-526-6

IMPRIMATUR
Bishop Ayo Maria Atoyebi, OP
Bishop Emeritus of Ilorin Diocese, Nigeria.

NIHIL OBSTAT
Very Rev. Fr. Stephen Audu
Ilorin Diocese,
Resident at St. Peter and All Hallow's Catholic Church,
Sacramento, California, USA.

*****

EDITOR
Lisa Timms
Senior Manager Operations, British Airways Plc.
Our Lady of Peace Parish, Burnham, UK.

*****

REFERENCES

The Holy Bible, Revised Standard Version, second Catholic Edition, Ignatian Press, San Francisco, 2006.

New International Version **(NIV).** *Holy Bible, New International Version®*, NIV® Copyright ©1973, 1978, 1984, 2011 by Biblica.Inc.

David Guzik's Enduring Word Bible Commentary (2018) enduringword.com

*****

Printed by:
Floreat Systems
Catholic Archdiocese of Benin Printing Press
30, Airport Road,
Benin City, Edo State, Nigeria
08133967455

I have a Heavenly Father who
sees it all, who cares for me
and who wants to help.

I am surrounded by saints in heaven
to whom I can turn for prayer.

I have the Holy Spirit within me.

I am a wounded helper. I choose joy

Dedicated to all the Catholic
Kenyans in the UK,
for all the love shown to me and
for making me one of them.

The children are happy & healthy and
live a free and play-filled childhood.
They are part of a rich network of
cousins and friends and do many
activities and trips of interest.
They can cook, forage & live close to
nature.

They learn through singing.
I am merely the gardener. Jesus
you call them into life.

FOREWORD

It is not easy to write book on daily reflections for seven days, never mind 365 days! Ever since the Lord Jesus Christ called me into a personal relationship with Him twenty-seven years ago - and the best decision I've ever made in life was to say yes to His call - I've gone through my fair share of books on daily reflections and there are only a handful that I would describe as truly God-breathed.

Daily reflection books are supposed to be life companions. The readers should hear God speak to them as they meditate on the Scripture passages and reflections. Moreover, the same Scripture passages and reflections should provide new insight, understanding and direction in subsequent years that is completely different from what was gained in previous years. Of course, that is the Holy Spirit at work bringing new inspiration and understanding to us as children of God when we read and reflect on His Word through His anointing on the writer. I can testify to numerous occasions when the words in the daily reflection books I read have been an exact confirmation of a word that the Holy Spirit already revealed to me during my quiet time of prayer. These are the daily reflection books that I call God-breathed because those occasions have transformed my walk with God and *Only Say the Word* falls into this category.

From the moment you pick up a book written by Fr. Emmanuel Gukena Okami you know you are in for a spiritual roller coaster ride. I have known Fr. Emmanuel for a relatively short period of time, but I can confidently describe him as a "man after God's own heart". His love for God and serving the people of God is unparalleled. He is an inspirational priest, pastor and a great teacher, one who not only encourages his flock but inspires all who come into contact with him to reach for greater heights in their faith, hope and love for God and the things of God. I am sure those of you who have met him will attest to this and it is that anointing on his life that is reflected in this book.

Only Say the Word is beautifully written with short Scripture passages and reflections that give the reader the opportunity to focus on a succinct theme for each day, thereby making it easier to deeply meditate on the Word of God and to hear God speak. Each day's reflection also includes a short daily prayer that enriches the reflection and helps the reader to pray in line with God's will for their lives that day. Another aspect of *Only Say the Word* is its ability to help the reader memorise Scriptures.

The Scripture passages are short and sweet, indeed sweeter than honey (Psalm 19:10) and if you are finding it difficult to memorise Scripture then the reflections in this book are perfect, as they will help you in that quest. You can go back and chew on the Word again and again throughout the day until it is rooted in your heart.

Only Say the Word is a power-packed daily reflection book. Do not let the cover fool you and don't be put off by its simplicity. In the pages of this reflection book you will hear God speak to you throughout the year and will be amazed by the power in the Word of God to encourage, strengthen, renew and give you wisdom to step into each day with abundant faith and trust in our Lord Jesus. To get the most out of it, I would encourage you to read it daily, meditatively and prayerfully. If you are ready to be transformed then dive in and ask the Lord Jesus to "only say the word" that will heal your soul each day, every day for the next 365 days!

Yoofi Clarke
Diocesan Service Team,
Catholic Charismatic Renewal, Northampton Diocese
St. Barnabas Cluster of Parishes, Milton Keynes, UK.

*****

AUTHOR'S NOTE

In the Gospel account of Matthew 4:1-11, we have the narrative of the temptation of Jesus by the devil. Three times the devil tempted Him and three times He overcame the temptations, drawing strength from the power and truth of the Word of God.

The Word of God is a very powerful tool that God has given to us, not just to overcome the devil but as an assurance of His promise, as a book containing saving truth, as wisdom to order our lives, as a guide in the journey of life, as a weapon of spiritual warfare, and as a means of accessing God's thought and will.

St. Paul tells us that *the Scripture is inspired by God and is useful for teaching, for reproof, for correction, and training in righteousness, so that everyone who belongs to God may be proficient, equipped for every good work* (2 Timothy 3:16-17).

It is in recognition of the power of the Word of God and propelled by the desire to support others who wish to drink deeply from this divine wellspring, that I undertake to write this book titled *Only Say the Word*.

Only Say the Word contains 365 Bible verses/quotes and a brief meditation on each. It is meant to be used for reflection on each day of the year.

The meditations are intentionally brief and are meant to inspire a holy thought in the heart of the reader. This will then culminate into a deeper contemplation, and in this way, the Word of God can sanctify our hearts and occupy our minds as we face the challenges of each new day.

The overall vision is to make the book a meditative guide for use throughout the year and to help bring people closer to the Lord through His Word by the power of the Holy Spirit.

I must confess that I am happy and grateful to the Holy Spirit for the inspiration, motivation and grace to write and complete this book. I was initially worried about the possibility of realising this project and completing it in good time but to the glory of God, it was written and completed within an incredibly short period.

I appreciate my editor and friend Lisa, my brother Yoofi who wrote the foreword, Ojochide Favour (my secretary), all those who reviewed the book and all those who contributed in significant ways to make this book possible.

I pray that as we journey through the year pondering on these divine teachings and promises, we may grow into maturity in the Spirit and we may be blessed through obedience to God's Word.

Yours in His vineyard,

Fr. Emmanuel Baraka-Gukena Okami
A Priest of Ilorin Diocese, Nigeria.
On Mission in Northampton Diocese, UK.
Word of Life Ministry (WOLM), Milton Keynes, UK.

*****

REVIEWS

This book, *Only Say the Word* by Fr. Emmanuel Okami, is a faith builder that provides a daily guide to God's Word and encourages one on a deeper walk through God's plan and purpose for your life. If you desire a closer relationship with God, then this is a must read as it gives an opportunity to expand your faith and awaken your inner life.

Aniekpeno Erhabor
Brainfill Academy, Nigeria.
Parishioner of St. Peter Catholic Church,
Hatfield, UK.

*****

The title *Only Say the Word* evokes the image of our need for humility and total submission whenever we approach the Word of God. In this state we are most able to absorb these spirit guided readings and rich practical reflections, written by Fr. Emmanuel Okami, and so there is nothing stopping our connection with God every day through the

Scriptures. Lord, open the eyes of our hearts as we read and may you continue to bless your servant, Fr. Emmanuel Okami.

J. Candy
Parishioner of St. Barnabas Cluster,
Milton Keynes, UK.

*****

As the year unfolds, may this valuable resource, *Only Say the Word,* written by Fr. Emmanuel Gukena Okami be your companion and may the Word of Christ in all its richness find a home in you. Reflecting on God's Word, as guided by Fr. Emmanuel, has helped me begin to appreciate the Scriptures, illuminating those areas of my life where I meet with difficulty or challenge. It has helped me to celebrate when I have experienced moments of understanding and joy. It is my hope that this book of reflection and prayer, will offer you a message of faith, hope and strength to help you lead the most fulfilling life possible. *Only Say the Word* is a gem. Keep it handy -its principles are timeless.

In all thy ways acknowledge Him, and He shall direct thy paths (Proverbs 3:6).

Catherine Waweru
Parishioner of Holy Redeemer Catholic Church,
Wexham, UK.

Only Say the Word is a series of short reflections for 365 days of the year written by Rev. Fr. Emmanuel Okami (a priest of the Catholic Diocese of Ilorin, Nigeria). It is written in simple words with a direct message for anyone who wants to journey with the Lord throughout the year. Each day has its own 'carefully selected' Bible verse, reflection and prayer. This is a book worthy of recommendation for both individuals and families. What a handy spiritual guide for an inspiring spiritual journey!

Rev. Fr. Shola Ajayi
Principal, St. Joseph Centenary Catholic College,
Ilorin, Nigeria.

*****

I must express my sincere appreciation of this beautiful treasure to humanity *Only Say the Word,* written by a profound and meticulous writer, Rev. Fr. Emmanuel Okami, who has never failed in giving, sacrificing and sharing his gifts of thoughts and writings to the world at large. Reading through these 365 days of reflections, I see it as a compass that will guide, shape and transform our lives as believers, as we prepare towards our Heavenly home.

In this beautiful treasure, the author begins the daily reflections with the assurance of God's uncon-ditional love and care for us. God invites us to commit our plans and purposes and cast all our worries unto Him, because He cares for us. This assurance of God's care for us gives us a guarantee of trust to believe in whatever situation we find ourselves in, to believe that the plans He has for us are for our welfare and for us to be happy here and with Him at the end of our journey.

As a pragmatist and a realist, Fr. Okami uses very simple language to explain the short reflections which include Bible quotations to meditate upon daily. This style is unique, and that uniqueness remains unassailable. Under the guidance of the Holy Spirit, Fr. Okami has given us a handy compass and tool to guide every day of our lives and bring us closer to God. I call on all of us to appreciate this good work and make it our own as we read and study it daily.

Let us therefore not doubt the power of God, let nothing shake our faith because God is loving and patient. He is always eager to pardon us and turn our mourning into rejoicing. Faith enables us to believe without doubting whatever God has revealed. Hence, we should not be anxious or disturbed by whatever God has begun in us because He will bring it to a worthy fulfilment.

Rev. Fr. Gabriel Odunaiya
Youth Chaplain, Archdiocese of Lagos, Nigeria.

*****

Thank you Fr. Emmanuel Baraka Gukena Okami for this lovely book *Only Say the Word*. This book has really motivated me to stay close to God, listen to His voice, and lean in close to His heart. It makes me want to hear what He has to say and gives me a renewed desire to live with His will as my will. Reading this book has made me realise that l am not sufficient, and it gives me relief to know I need to depend on God alone.

The reflections, based on daily Scripture verses, have really made me deepen my understanding of the Bible. The verses are easy to understand, and it is suitable for different age groups. This book reminds me that the Holy Spirit gives us the right words when we need them.

I would highly recommend this book to anyone who would like to read and reflect on the Word of God, especially when you're facing a challenge. Remember, the Word of God can lift your spirits and give you guidance for a fresh start.

Janepher Minai
Parishioner of Holy Ghost Catholic Church,
Luton, UK.

*****

Words cannot do justice to this inspirational book, in which you find daily prayers and readings at hand. The prayers are simple and easy to relate with and each day brings a new uplifting Scripture reading. Whenever you feel compelled and heavy burdened by everyday life, you have this positive and encouraging book to turn to. The daily reflections are short and sweet, and the simplicity of this book makes it so inspirational. My prayer is whoever reads this little book will be truly blessed with everyday devotions. This book can be related to by both adults and children. I am thankful for these fantastic, word filled, Holy Spirit led reflections. God bless you all very much.

Mrs Joyce Waithera Mburu
St. Cedd's Catholic Church, Ilford, UK.

*****

ONLY SAY THE
WORD

365 Days Of Reflection On The Word Of God

FR. EMMANUEL GUKENA OKAMI

TABLE OF CONTENTS

JANUARY

Day 1	1 Peter 5:7	God cares about you	2
Day 2	Psalm 27:4	What are your priorities?	3
Day 3	Philippians 4:13	You are not weak	4
Day 4	Jeremiah 29:11	God has a plan for you	5
Day 5	2 Timothy 1:7	The Spirit of power is in you	6
Day 6	Galatians 3:26-27	Put on Christ	7
Day 7	Genesis 13:8	Sacrifice for peace	8
Day 8	Exodus 3:4-5	Remove your sandals	9
Day 9	Revelation 2:4-5	What about your initial love?	10
Day 10	Deuteronomy 22:1	Concern for others	11
Day 11	Colossians 1:9-10	Knowledge of God's will	12
Day 12	Ephesians 4:15	Speak the truth in love	13
Day 13	2 Corinthians 3:5	Avoid boasting	14
Day 14	Judges 6:15-16	When God is with you	15
Day 15	Job 35:6-7	We add nothing to His greatness	16
Day 16	Psalm 31:15	My times are in your hands	17
Day 17	Proverbs 25:21	No room for retaliation	18
Day 18	Zechariah 2:8	Apple of God's eye	19
Day 19	Jeremiah 7:8-10	False hope in God's promises	20
Day 20	John 8:11	I have not come to condemn you	21
Day 21	Matthew 24:13	Those who endured to the last	22
Day 22	Psalm 138:2	He honoured His name	23

Day 23	James 3:13	Wisdom proven through good life	24
Day 24	James 4:14-15	Appreciate today	25
Day 25	1Thessalonians 4:3-5	Control your body in nominees and honour	26
Day 26	Luke 1:37	With Him all things are possible	27
Day 27	Isaiah 43:1	You are mine	28
Day 28	Philippians 1:21	Death is gain	29
Day 29	Philippians 2:3	Examine your intention	30
Day 30	Exodus 20:7	God's name	31
Day 31	Leviticus 20:6	Religious purity	32

FEBRUARY

Day 1	Numbers 14:8	Right living honours God	34
Day 2	Exodus 11:7	God knows those who serve Him	35
Day 3	Exodus 20:3	Have no other god	36
Day 4	Deuteronomy 1:6	You have stayed too long	37
Day 5	Mark 4:41	Even nature obeys Him	38
Day 6	1 Kings 3:9	Wisdom to govern	39
Day 7	Nehemiah 8:10	The joy of the Lord	40
Day 8	Tobit 4:7-8	Generosity to the needy	41
Day 9	Psalm 31:24	Those who wait on the Lord	42
Day 10	James 5:12	Let your yes be yes	43
Day 11	Daniel 12:3	The virtuous will shine	44
Day 12	Luke 6:37	You are not a judge	45
Day 13	Ephesians 3:20	He is able	46
Day 14	Deuteronomy 31:6	I will not forsake you	47
Day 15	Hebrews 12:2	Focus on Jesus	48
Day 16	2 Corinthians 5:10	We shall render an account	49
Day 17	2 Corinthians 6:18	I will be a Father to you	50
Day 18	Hebrews 12:1	Lay aside encumbrances	51
Day 19	2 Corinthians 5:7	We walk by faith	52

Day 20   Philippians 4:4   Rejoice in the Lord   53
Day 21   Titus 3:2   Courtesy towards all people   54
Day 22   Titus 3:1   Lead by example   55
Day 23   Titus 1:7   A model of good deeds   56
Day 24   Exodus 33:17   Walking in faith and obedience 57
Day 25   Numbers 30:2   Fulfil your vows to the Lord   58
Day 26   1 Samuel 20:17   Jonathan, a true friend   59
Day 27   2 Samuel 7:18   It's time to be grateful   60
Day 28   2 Kings 20:5   He is a merciful God   61
Day 29   1Thessalonians 5:18 Give thanks in all
(for a leap year)   circumstances   62

MARCH

Day 1   Isaiah 40:31   Those who wait on the Lord   64
Day 2   1 Corinthians 16:13 Stand firm in your faith   65
Day 3   Jonah 4:10-11   The supremacy of loving
                               the human person   66
Day 4   John 15:13   No greater love   67
Day 5   Joshua 1:7   Success in obedience   68
Day 6   Romans 8:28   All things are working for good 69
Day 7   Habakkuk 3:17-18   Yet, I will rejoice   70
Day 8   Philippians 3:7   To find Jesus is to
                               find everything   71
Day 9   Psalm 23:4   Even though I walk through   72
Day 10   Matthew 6:33   Seek first   73
Day 11   Genesis 22:8   God will provide   74
Day 12   Galatians 5:1   Christ has set you free   75
Day 13   Numbers 13:30   Positive spirit   76
Day 14   Colossians 3:5-8   Put to death   77
Day 15   Leviticus 19:18   No room for vengeance   78
Day 16   Philippians 2:14-15 Be a shining example   79
Day 17   Ruth 1:16   The faithfulness of Ruth   80
Day 18   Luke 10:5   Be an ambassador of peace   81
Day 19   Mark 10:13-14   Ministering to children   82

Day 20	Romans 8:31	If God is for us	83
Day 21	Lamentations3:22-23	They are new every morning	84
Day 22	2 Corinthians 4:17	Eternal weight of glory	85
Day 23	Proverbs 3:5-6	Do not rely on your insight	86
Day 24	Hebrews 11:6	Impossible to please God without faith	87
Day 25	Psalm 30:5	His anger is for a moment	88
Day 26	1 John 3:1	You are a child of God	89
Day 27	Genesis 37:4	Avoid hatred	90
Day 28	1Thessalonians 5:4	You are not in the darkness	91
Day 29	Philippians 1:6	He will bring it to completion	92
Day 30	Exodus 18:24	Be open to good counsel	93
Day 31	Matthew 21:21-22	Ask in faith	94

APRIL

Day 1	Romans 8:38-39	Nothing can separate us from His love	96
Day 2	Proverbs 17:22	Christians are to be cheerful	97
Day 3	Ephesians 3:17	Be rooted in love	98
Day 4	Genesis 26:12	God's blessing makes a difference	99
Day 5	1 Peter 2:9	Your identity in Christ	100
Day 6	Isaiah 12:2	God is my salvation	101
Day 7	Mark 12:30	You shall love the Lord	102
Day 8	Numbers 23:20	When God blesses you	103
Day 9	1 Peter 2:11	Abstain from desires of the flesh	104
Day 10	Job 42:10	A testimony is on the way	105
Day 11	Luke 20:25	Give to God, what is God's	106
Day 12	1Thessalonians 5:14	Be patient with the weak	107
Day 13	Ephesians 2:4-5	God is rich in mercy	108
Day 14	1 Kings 10:9	Be a blessing	109
Day 15	Colossians 3:17	Do everything in the name of the Lord	110

Day 16	Hebrews 9:27	Death is once	111
Day 17	Colossians 4:6	Let your speech be gracious	112
Day 18	Psalm 20:7	Our pride is in God's name	113
Day 19	1 Samuel 15:22	Obedience is better than sacrifice	114
Day 20	Philippians 3:12	I press on	115
Day 21	Exodus 3:7	The God who observes	116
Day 22	Matthew 11:6	Take no offence in the Lord	117
Day 23	2 Peter 2:20	Do not return to sin	118
Day 24	Ephesians 4:8	He gave gifts to people	119
Day 25	Leviticus 19:16	Be careful what you sow	120
Day 26	James 1:2-4	Joy in trials	121
Day 27	Deuteronomy 30:20	Hold fast to the Lord	122
Day 28	2 Chronicles 7:14	Turn to Him in repentance	123
Day 29	Proverbs 10:12	Love covers offences	124
Day 30	Romans 14:7	We do not live for ourselves	125

MAY

Day 1	Ephesians 6:10	Be strong in the Lord	127
Day 2	1 Corinthians 15:58	Be steadfast and excel in God's work	128
Day 3	Deuteronomy 20:4	God will fight for you	129
Day 4	Ezra 1:1	God moved people for His purpose	130
Day 5	1 Corinthians 10:12	Watch that you do not fall	131
Day 6	Exodus 14:13-14	The Egyptians you see today	132
Day 7	Romans 15:1	We are not to please ourselves	133
Day 8	2Corinthians 12:9-10	My Grace is sufficient for you	134
Day 9	Hebrews 10:23	He who has promised is faithful	135
Day 10	Romans 12:12	Rejoice in hope	136
Day 11	Matthew 6:34	Do not worry about tomorrow	137
Day 12	Galatians 6:9	Do not grow weary of doing what is right	138

Day 13	Acts 3:6	Something more than silver or gold	139
Day 14	1 Corinthians 10:13	No temptation beyond your strength	140
Day 15	John 14:27	Peace I give you	141
Day 16	Romans 12:18	Live peaceably with all	142
Day 17	Hebrews 11:1	Faith is the conviction of what is unseen	143
Day 18	Romans 12:19	Vengeance is mine	144
Day 19	Acts 7:55-56	I see heaven opened	145
Day 20	1Thessalonians 5:16	Rejoice always	146
Day 21	Romans 13:2	Rebellion ruins spirituality	147
Day 22	Ephesians 4:22	Put away your old self	148
Day 23	Exodus 20:16	No false witness	149
Day 24	Jeremiah 29:10	God will fulfil His promise in His time	150
Day 25	Nehemiah 1:5	Covenant keeping God	151
Day 26	Proverbs 30:5	Every word of God is true	152
Day 27	1Thessalonians 5:22	Abstain from evil	153
Day 28	Genesis 18:14	Nothing that the Lord cannot do	154
Day 29	Colossians 2:6-7	Be rooted and built up in Christ	155
Day 30	Joshua 10:12-13	The prayer of faith	156
Day 31	Ephesians 4:2-3	The unity of the Spirit	157

JUNE

Day 1	1Thessalonians 5:17	Pray without ceasing	159
Day 2	2 Corinthians 3:5	Our competence is from God	160
Day 3	Romans 13:7	Honour to whom honour is due	161
Day 4	Ephesians 4:1	A life worthy of your call	162
Day 5	Romans 12:2	Do not be conformed to the world	163
Day 6	1 Corinthians 10:24	Act for the good of others	164
Day 7	Genesis 6:9	The example of Noah	165

Day 8	Colossians 3:23-24	Serve the Lord through your work	166
Day 9	Exodus 19:5-6	You will be a treasured possession	167
Day 10	Job 5:17	The discipline of the Almighty	168
Day 11	Proverbs 10:2-3	Ill-gotten treasures	169
Day 12	2 Corinthians 9:7	God loves a cheerful giver	170
Day 13	Amos 5:14	Seek no evil	171
Day 14	Leviticus 19:17	Do not share in anyone's guilt	172
Day 15	Joshua 24:15	I will serve the Lord	173
Day 16	1Thessalonians 2:4-5	To please God is our goal	174
Day 17	Romans 12:9	Let love be genuine	175
Day 18	Judges 16:18	The spirit of Delilah	176
Day 19	Nehemiah 1:11	Talk to God first	177
Day 20	Psalm 4:7	God is the giver of true joy	178
Day 21	Numbers 5:5-7	The Lord cares how we treat others	179
Day 22	1 Kings 12:13-14	Wrong counsel	180
Day 23	Galatians 5:16	Live by the Spirit	181
Day 24	Ecclesiastes 7:21-22	Do not give heed to everything you hear	182
Day 25	Leviticus 18:1-3	The sin of conformity	183
Day 26	Romans 14:13	Put no stumbling block	184
Day 27	1 Samuel 1:10-11	Hannah brought her pains to God	185
Day 28	Joshua 1:8	Ponder on God's Word	186
Day 29	Malachi 3:18	It is not useless to serve the Lord	187
Day 30	Genesis 39:7-9	Fear God, respect people	188

JULY

Day 1	Ephesians 6:20	Ambassador of God	190
Day 2	Ephesians 6:6	Do what is right always	191
Day 3	Ephesians 6:12	Spiritual warfare	192

Day 4	Romans 14:19	Seek Peace	193
Day 5	Romans 15:2	Seek the wellbeing of others	194
Day 6	1 Corinthians 13:4-6	Qualities of love	195
Day 7	2 Corinthians 6:18	I will be a Father to you	196
Day 8	John 14:18	I won't leave you as orphans	197
Day 9	Galatians 6:7	You reap what you sow	198
Day 10	Proverbs 19:2	Do not rush to act	199
Day 11	Ephesians 4:15	Walk as a wise person	200
Day 12	Ephesians 2:19	Your special place in God's family	201
Day 13	Colossians 2:8	Be careful of empty deceit	202
Day 14	Colossians 3:16	Let the word of God dwell richly in you	203
Day 15	2Thessalonians 3:13	Do not be tired of doing good	204
Day 16	Genesis 39:19-20	Be not hasty to believe	205
Day 17	Exodus 19:14	Prepare yourself	206
Day 18	Exodus 20:15	Do not steal	207
Day 19	Exodus 20:17	Against covetousness	208
Day 20	Leviticus 19:3	Honouring our parents	209
Day 21	Job 33:4	God's breath is in you	210
Day 22	Job 22:21	Agree with God	211
Day 23	Psalm 50:15	Call on me in trouble	212
Day 24	Psalm 42:5	Your soul should not be downcast	213
Day 25	Psalm 19:14	May my words be acceptable	214
Day 26	Hosea 6:4	Love like a morning cloud	215
Day 27	Hosea 10:1	Do not be distracted by blessing	216
Day 28	Malachi 3:6	God doesn't change	217
Day 29	Zechariah 13:1	Fountain of mercy	218
Day 30	Zechariah 10:1	Be bold to ask	219
Day 31	Isaiah 6:1	The Lord is on the throne	220

AUGUST

Day 1	1Thessalonians 5:6	Be awake	222
Day 2	Isaiah 58:9-10	Your light will rise in darkness	223
Day 3	2 Corinthians 5:15	We live for Him	224
Day 4	Haggai 1:7-9	Consider how you have fared	225
Day 5	Proverbs 6:9-11	Laziness	226
Day 6	Judges 6:13	The Lord is with you	227
Day 7	Jeremiah 18:6	You are the potter, I am the clay	228
Day 8	Exodus 4:13-14	Lord, send someone else	229
Day 9	1 Peter 1:3-4	An imperishable inheritance	230
Day 10	2 Kings 5:16	It's not all about money	231
Day 11	Romans 12:3	Do not think too highly of yourself	232
Day 12	Leviticus 20:7	Be holy as I am holy	233
Day 13	Ephesians 1:13	Marked by the seal of the Spirit	234
Day 14	2Thessalonians 3:7-8	Do not be a burden to anyone	235
Day 15	Job 22:25-26	God is my gold	236
Day 16	Psalm 46:1-3	God is our refuge	237
Day 17	Ephesians 1:4	Chosen before the world was made	238
Day 18	Ephesians 4:25	The truth in love	239
Day 19	Romans 12:15	Rejoice with those who rejoice	240
Day 20	Deuteronomy 6:14	God deserves all your attention	241
Day 21	Hebrews 8:12	I will remember their sins no more	242
Day 22	Proverbs 4:23-24	Keep your heart with vigilance	243
Day 23	Songs 2:4	His banner over me is love	244
Day 24	Romans 12:17	Do not pay back with evil	245
Day 25	Sirach 7:1-2	Stay away from wrong	246
Day 26	2 Corinthians 7:1	Purification from spiritual defilement	247
Day 27	2 Samuel 9:6-7	Show kindness	248
Day 28	Psalm 24:1	The Lord's is the earth	249

Day 29	3 John 1:5	Kindness to strangers	250
Day 30	Romans 13:8-9	The debt of love	251
Day 31	Judges 6:6	They cried to the Lord	252

SEPTEMBER

Day 1	Ezekiel 18:24	Living on past glory	254
Day 2	1Thessalonians 5:21	Test everything	255
Day 3	2 Corinthians 4:7	Treasure in clay jars	256
Day 4	Genesis 1:27	Created in His image	257
Day 5	Ephesians 2:10	Created for good works	258
Day 6	Deuteronomy 7:7	You are special because He chose you	259
Day 7	Tobit 12:9-10	Self-enemies	260
Day 8	Sirach 9:10	Do not forget your true friends	261
Day 9	Jude 1:5	He is merciful and just	262
Day 10	James 4:6	He gives grace to the humble	263
Day 11	John 10:10	Abundance of life is in Jesus alone	264
Day 12	2 Peter 1:5-6	The supplements to faith	265
Day 13	Isaiah 49:24-25	Captives from the mighty	266
Day 14	Genesis 30:27	A carrier of blessing	267
Day 15	James 1:12	The crown of life	268
Day 16	1 John 1:8-9	He forgives if we confess	269
Day 17	Jude 1:21	Keep yourself in God's love	270
Day 18	Nahum 1:3	He doesn't clear the guilty	271
Day 19	Romans 10:17	Faith comes through hearing	272
Day 20	2 Timothy 1:7	Not a spirit of cowardice	273
Day 21	John 14:26	The Holy Spirit will teach you	274
Day 22	Colossians 1:13-14	Rescued from the power of darkness	275
Day 23	Galatians 5:22	The fruit of the Spirit	276
Day 24	1 Corinthians 1:1-3	In the absence of love	277
Day 25	Job 4:6	Fear of the Lord	278

Day 26   Exodus 1:17   Obedience to God first   279
Day 27   John 16:8   The Spirit will convict
                            and reveal   280
Day 28   James 1:2-4   Faith in trials   281
Day 29   Amos 5:6   Seek the Lord and live   282
Day 30   Proverbs 1:8-9   Honour your parents   283

OCTOBER

Day 1   John 1:34   Called to testify   285
Day 2   Romans 14:23   Our faith is the canon   286
Day 3   2 Timothy 2:20   Vessels for special use   287
Day 4   1 John 3:8   To destroy the work of the devil 288
Day 5   Romans 9:30   The Lord wants all to be saved 289
Day 6   John 4:48   Faith not based on signs   290
Day 7   Exodus 4:12   I will teach you what to speak 291
Day 8   Isaiah 45:19   You won't seek me in vain   292
Day 9   Hebrews 11:1   Faith is conviction   293
Day 10   John 11:40   You will see the glory of God 294
Day 11   Revelation 12:11 The conquerors   295
Day 12   Daniel 11:32   Loyalty will be tested   296
Day 13   Psalm 14:1   Atheism is foolishness   297
Day 14   Ephesians 6:14-15 The armour of spiritual warfare 298
Day 15   Joshua 7:12   Unless we rely totally on God 299
Day 16   Matthew 5:9   The peacemakers   300
Day 17   1 Timothy 6:12   Fight the good fight   301
Day 18   1 Peter 3:13   1 Peter 3:13   302
Day 19   Isaiah 57:15   God dwells with the humble
                            and contrite   303
Day 20   Psalm 33:11   The counsel of the Lord
                            stands firm   304
Day 21   2 Corinthians 6:2 At an acceptable time   305
Day 22   Romans 9:15   Do not take mercy for granted 306
Day 23   1 Peter 2:9   We are a chosen race   307
Day 24   Isaiah 3:10   The innocent are fortunate   308

Day 25	Daniel 6:22	The angels, our protectors	309
Day 26	Proverbs 28:1	The righteous is bold	310
Day 27	1 Peter 4:1	Suffering in the flesh	311
Day 28	Jeremiah 31:35-36	The Almighty has promised	312
Day 29	Mark 13:31	My words will not pass away	313
Day 30	Ezekiel 3:18	The watchtower	314
Day 31	Philippians 4:19	God will supply your needs	315

NOVEMBER

Day 1	Revelation 21:8	The second death	317
Day 2	2 Timothy 4:1-2	Proclaim the message	318
Day 3	Philippians 2:9	Name above all names	319
Day 4	Proverbs 18:10	The name of the Lord is a strong tower	320
Day 5	Ecclesiastes 5:10-11	The lover of money	321
Day 6	John 6:54	Eat my flesh	322
Day 7	John 15:16	I chose you	323
Day 8	Joel 2:32	Salvation for those who trust	324
Day 9	2 Peter 3:11	Living holy and godly lives	325
Day 10	Luke 12:15	Be on your guard against greed	326
Day 11	Zechariah 4:6	It is not by might	327
Day 12	Matthew 4:4	Not by bread alone	328
Day 13	Psalm 19:7	The Law of the Lord is perfect	329
Day 14	Matthew 1:21c	His name is Jesus	330
Day 15	Isaiah 26:3	Peace for those who trust	331
Day 16	Psalm 66:18	Cherish no iniquity in your heart	332
Day 17	Mark 11:22b-23	Pray without doubting	333
Day 18	Romans 13:12	Put on the armour of light	334
Day 19	Titus 2:11-12	Renounce impiety and worldly passion	335
Day 20	Titus 2:14	Zealous for good deeds	336
Day 21	John 15:4	Abide in me	337
Day 22	Psalm 125:2	The Lord surrounds His people	338
Day 23	Mark 7:23	The state of your heart	339

Day 24	Matthew 5:48	Just as your heavenly Father	340
Day 25	1 Corinthians 10:9	Do not put the Lord to the test	341
Day 26	Psalm 34:10	Those who seek the Lord	342
Day 27	Ecclesiastes 9:11	The race is not to the swift	343
Day 28	John 14:15	Obedience is the proof of love	344
Day 29	Psalm 137:5-6	If I forget Jerusalem	345
Day 30	Acts 10:4	God sees your good deeds	346

DECEMBER

Day 1	John 14:6	Jesus is the way	348
Day 2	1 Chronicles 4:10	The Lord answered Jabez	349
Day 3	1 John 2:1-2	We have an advocate with the Father	350
Day 4	Luke 18:14b	Exaltation through humility	351
Day 5	Ephesians 3:20	He is able to do more	352
Day 6	John 1:4	In Him is life	353
Day 7	1 Peter 4:9	Be hospitable	354
Day 8	John 5:36	The works that I do	355
Day 9	Psalm 18:3	He is worthy to be praised	356
Day 10	Isaiah 42:8	My glory I give to no other	357
Day 11	Luke 6:38	Be generous	358
Day 12	Psalm 20:1-2	May He answer you	359
Day 13	Matthew 5:1	Let your light shine	360
Day 14	Luke 12:1-2	Beware of hypocrisy	361
Day 15	Genesis 17:1-2	Walk before me and be blameless	362
Day 16	1 Samuel 15:23	Disobedience is rebellion	363
Day 17	Mark 9:9	Tell no one	364
Day 18	John 6:66-68	Do you also wish to go away?	365
Day 19	Ezekiel 36:24	Heaven is our true home	366
Day 20	Psalm 40:1	I waited patiently	367
Day 21	Matthew 8:2-3	He touched the untouchable	368
Day 22	James 4:7	Resist the devil	369

Day 23	James 4:8	Draw near to God	370
Day 24	John 12:26	Whoever serves me must follow me	371
Day 25	2 Corinthians 6:14	Be not mismatched with unbelievers	372
Day 26	Psalm 25:9	Humility brings blessing	373
Day 27	Isaiah 59:1-2	His hands are not too short	374
Day 28	Isaiah 1:18	Come now	375
Day 29	1 Peter 1:2	Chosen by the Father	376
Day 30	1 Corinthians 15:58	Your labour is not in vain	377
Day 31	Ecclesiastes 12:14	Every deed shall be judged	378

*****

JANUARY

GOD CARES ABOUT YOU

⁷ Cast all your anxiety on Him,
because He cares for you.
1 Peter 5:7

Reflection

Dear Child of God, the Lord says, "He cares about us." He is genuinely concerned about what we are going through, and He is willing to help us. Keep in mind this day that we are not alone, unloved or left without any support. We should not allow our burdens to crush us. Remember that the Lord wants us to bring them to Him and we will never have to go through it all by ourselves. Even if people are indifferent to our plight, our loving Father is not.

PRAYER

Lord Jesus, I bring my needs before you today. May I always keep in mind that you care for me and that I am never alone. With you by my side, it is well with me.

Amen.

Day 2

WHAT ARE YOUR PRIORITIES?

---

*⁴One thing I asked of the Lord, that will
I seek after: to live in the house of
the Lord all the days of my life,
to behold the beauty of the Lord, and to
inquire in His temple.*
Psalm 27:4

Reflection

Dear Child of God, what are the things that are important to us? What do we ask for? What do we need? What do we desperately want God to do for us? Are we asking God for things that will make our relationship with Him better and stronger? Are we asking for things that are important for our salvation?

Like the Psalmist, let us place as our priority, things that will strengthen our relationship with God and aid our eternal salvation. To dwell eternally in God's presence should be our highest aspiration.

PRAYER

Lord Jesus, teach me to know the value of the passing things of this world that I may seek the things of eternal value.
Amen.

3

YOU ARE NOT WEAK

¹³I can do all things through Him who strengthens me.
Philippians 4:13

Reflection

Dear Child of God, keep in mind today that we are not weak, powerless or failures. We are capable of anything God wants us to do. The strength may not be within, but it is supplied from above. We must not be too quick to say we can't because if God asks us to do it, He will supply the strength.

PRAYER

Lord Jesus, I confess that I can do all things. I rely on your power and your grace and I know I will not fail.
Amen.

Day 4
GOD HAS A PLAN FOR YOU

"For surely I know the plans I have for you, says the Lord, plans for your welfare and not for harm, to give you a future with hope.
Jeremiah 29:11

Reflection

Dear Child of God, our lives are not lived according to chance or accident of nature. God has a plan for us. Each of us is part of His plan and His plans for us are good. Yes, they may not be clear to us at the moment but when we learn to trust and walk with Him in obedience, He is preparing a future full of hope for us. Sometimes He may take us through the wilderness, but our destination will be glorious.

PRAYER

Lord Jesus, I trust and surrender to you. I know you have a plan for my life, and I embrace with joy whatever is your plan for me. I know for sure that it is for my good.
Amen.

THE SPIRIT OF POWER IS IN YOU

*⁷for God did not give us a spirit of
cowardice, but rather a spirit of power
and of love and of self-discipline.*
2 Timothy 1:7

Reflection

Dear Child of God, the Spirit of God that we have received is a spirit of power, love and self-control. The more we learn to be attentive to the Holy Spirit and grow in our intimacy, the more we discover that we have within us the power to be bold, to love and to control the flesh. Let us therefore surrender to the Spirit of God within us to dispel our fears, our inclination to hate and our tendency to allow the flesh to dominate us.

PRAYER

Lord Jesus, I surrender to your Holy Spirit within me. Dispel every fear from my heart, every hatred of persons and every attraction to sin.
Amen.

Day 6
PUT ON CHRIST

*²⁶for in Christ Jesus you are all children
of God through faith. ²⁷As many
of you as were baptised into Christ have
clothed yourselves with Christ.*
Galatians 3:26-27

Reflection

Dear Child of God, by our baptism we have all become sons and daughters of God and we have become members of the larger family of God's people. Our old garment of sin has been put away and now we have put on Christ. Keep this in mind today: we are each members of God's family and we are putting on Christ. Let everyone who comes in contact with us see more of Christ and none of our old selves.

PRAYER

Lord Jesus, thank you for bringing me to your family of the redeemed. May you always be in my words, actions and thoughts and may you be visible to others through me.
Amen.

Day 7

SACRIFICE FOR PEACE

*⁸Then Abram said to Lot, "Let there be
no strife between you and me, and
between your herders and my herders; for
we are kindred."*
Genesis 13:8

Reflection

Dear Child of God, like Abram said to Lot, let us try
within our power to avoid unnecessary conflict,
argument, tension and strife between us and others.
Let us be bearers of peace. Sometimes peace demands
sacrifice from us, but it is more rewarding than
insisting on our right and orchestrating division and
strife.

PRAYER

Lord Jesus, help me to seek and work for peace
wherever I find myself.
Amen.

Day 8

REMOVE YOUR SANDALS

⁴When the Lord saw that he had turned aside to see, God called to him out of the bush, "Moses, Moses!" And he said, "Here I am." ⁵Then he said, "Come no closer! Remove the sandals from your feet, for the place on which you are standing is holy ground."
Exodus 3:4-5

Reflection

God called Moses through a strange sight. He demanded him to put away his sandals, a symbol of stain and filth, because He was standing before a Holy God. Dear Child of God, the Lord wants us to approach Him with all stains and filth put aside. Let us constantly examine our minds and carefully remove from our lives anything unbefitting of the holiness of God, whose presence fills the whole earth.

PRAYER

Lord Jesus, help me to see what I need to remove in my life so that I may stand in your presence with clean and clear conscience.
Amen.

WHAT ABOUT YOUR INITIAL LOVE?

⁴ But I have this against you, that you have abandoned the love you had at first.
⁵ Remember then from what you have fallen; repent and do the works you did at first. If not, I will come to you and remove your lampstand from its place, unless you repent.
Revelation 2:4-5

Reflection

The Lord reprimanded the members of the Church of Ephesus for abandoning the love they had at first. They started their relationship with God with so much zeal, love and dedication, but they allowed their zeal to gradually dwindle with the passage of time. God saw this and was unimpressed. Dear Child of God, let us examine our love for God. Is it growing, stagnant or reducing? Are we still burning in zeal for the Lord or have time and circumstances turned our initial fire to cold ashes? The Lord says wake up and surrender our ashes to be rekindled with new fire.

PRAYER

Lord Jesus, may my love for you not diminish. Give me oil in my lamp and keep me burning for love of you.
Amen.

Day 10

CONCERN FOR OTHERS

22 You shall not watch your neighbour's ox or sheep straying away and ignore them; you shall take them back to their owner.
Deuteronomy 22:1

Reflection

Dear Child of God, the Lord wants us to be concerned about others and be willing to help them. We are not to be indifferent or turn our eyes when we can do something to help someone prevent a danger or loss. Sometimes we may be misunderstood, criticised, judged wrongly or unappreciated, but what is most important is that we have acted in charity and in good faith.

PRAYER

Lord Jesus, teach me to be sensitive to the needs of those around me and be willing to give a helping hand to my neighbour without counting the cost.
Amen.

KNOWLEDGE OF GOD'S WILL

⁹ For this reason, since the day we heard it, we have not ceased praying for you and asking that you may be filled with the knowledge of God's will in all spiritual wisdom and understanding, ¹⁰ so that you may lead lives worthy of the Lord, fully pleasing to him, as you bear fruit in every good work and as you grow in the knowledge of God.
Colossians 1:9-10

Reflection

St. Paul prayed for the Colossians to be filled with the knowledge of God's will, to lead a life fully pleasing to the Lord, bearing fruit in every good work and increasing in the knowledge of the Lord.

Dear child of God, It is very important for us to also be able to discern God's will. When we know God's will for us, we have peace. However, to know God's will, we need to grow in the knowledge of God Himself. Let us therefore use every available spiritual means to seek to deepen our knowledge of the Lord and be determined to embrace whatever is His will for us.

PRAYER

Lord Jesus, help me to grow in the knowledge of the Father and to embrace whatever He wills for me.
Amen.

Day 12

SPEAK THE TRUTH IN LOVE

*15 But speaking the truth in love, we
must grow up in every way into Him
who is the head, into Christ*
Ephesians 4:15

Reflection

Dear Child of God, we have an obligation to always
speak the truth to ourselves and to others. However, it
is not enough to discern and speak the truth; it must
be spoken in love, in kindness, with the intention to
help and build the other person. We must not speak
the truth in a way that condemns anyone or presents
us as better than anyone. We are all weak, fallible and
imperfect, caught up in the struggle of becoming like
Christ, who alone is perfect.

PRAYER

Lord Jesus, teach me to be truthful always but
most importantly, help me first to love those to
whom I speak the truth.
Amen.

Day 13

AVOID BOASTING

*⁵Not that we are competent of ourselves
to claim anything as coming from us;
our competence is from God,*
2 Corinthians 3:5

Reflection

St. Paul reminds us that we owe everything good in us to Christ and so we should avoid all forms of boasting or looking down on others. Dear Child of God, when we recognise that God is to be praised for everything praiseworthy in us, we are able to render Him due honour and we dispose ourselves to be used by Him for greater exploit. Pride and self-glorification impede the operation of grace in us and obscure God's glory in us.

PRAYER

Lord Jesus, help me to be humble like you and to recognise that everything that is good in me has come from you.
Amen.

Day 14

WHEN GOD IS WITH YOU

15 He responded, "But sir, how can I deliver Israel? My clan is the weakest in Manasseh, and I am the least in my family." 16 The Lord said to him, "But I will be with you, and you shall strike down the Midianites, every one of them."

Judges 6:15-16

Reflection

The Lord commissioned Gideon to go and deliver Israel from the oppression of the Midianites. He immediately confessed his incompetence and unworthiness, however, God insisted that he should go and that He would be with him. Dear Child of God, when God sends us on any assignment, be sure He will be with us. When God is with us, we will not fail or be put to shame.

PRAYER

Lord Jesus, help me to grow in confidence that you are with me and that with you by my side, I can do whatever you want me to do.
Amen.

Day 15

WE ADD NOTHING TO HIS GREATNESS

⁶If you have sinned, what do you accomplish against him? And if your transgressions are multiplied, what do you do to him? ⁷If you are righteous, what do you give to him; or what does he receive from your hand?
Job 35:6-7

Reflection

Sometimes we are tempted to give up our righteousness because we think God has not treated us as we desire. Sometimes we also approach God counting on our merit and thinking we deserve something because we have been faithful. Dear Child of God, we do not reduce the glory and majesty of God by our unfaithfulness and He doesn't depend on our faithfulness to be or remain who He is. Our faithfulness helps us, not God and our unfaithfulness does no harm to God but to us. We can add nothing to His greatness, but we can grow in grace and welcome peace by choosing to be faithful.

PRAYER

Lord Jesus, help me never to be attracted to a life of unfaithfulness to you.
Amen.

Day 16
MY TIMES ARE IN YOUR HANDS

15 My times are in your hand; deliver me from the hand of my enemies and persecutors.
Psalm 31:15

Reflection
Dear Child of God, keep in mind that our times are in God's hands. He is the one in charge of our lives and He controls time and events. He will give us what we need at the right time and in His own way. So as we look to the Lord for any blessing, we should keep calm because the One who controls time and seasons, the One who governs the world, history and events, is our Father.

PRAYER
Lord Jesus, help me to keep calm and know that God will not refuse me what is good for me when the time is right.
Amen.

NO ROOM FOR RETALIATION

²¹ If your enemies are hungry, give them bread to eat; and if they are thirsty, give them water to drink
Proverbs 25:21

Reflection

Dear Child of God, the Lord does not want us to have a vengeful spirit or to nurse any passion for retaliation. The Lord wants us to preserve the goodness in us, no matter the ill treatment we endure from outside. Whenever someone who bears us ill needs our help, let us not withdraw from assisting. Everyone gives from the store within. A wicked person gives from the store of wickedness within and a good person gives goodness even to the undeserving because he can only give what he has got.

PRAYER

Lord Jesus, teach me to overcome the inclination to repay evil with evil. May I be charitable even to those who are unkind to me.
Amen.

Day 18
APPLE OF GOD'S EYE

*⁸ For thus said the Lord of hosts (after
His glory sent me) regarding the nations
that plundered you: Truly, one who
touches you touches the apple of my eye.*
Zechariah 2:8

Reflection

Dear Child of God, we should not listen to the voice
saying we are worthless, that we are not special or
worthy of love. We are all special to the Lord. We are
the apple of His eye, we are very important to Him and
He guards us jealously. We should rejoice in this
honour and celebrate ourselves as precious possessions
of God. When we know who we are to God, we will
silence the voice of the ancient deceiver.

PRAYER

Lord Jesus, help me to understand by the power
of the Holy Spirit that I am very dear to God and
He cares so much about me.
Amen.

FALSE HOPE IN GOD'S PROMISES

⁸ Here you are, trusting in deceptive words to no avail. ⁹ Will you steal, murder, commit adultery, swear falsely, make offerings to Baal, and go after other gods that you have not known, ¹⁰ and then come and stand before me in this house, which is called by my name, and say, "We are safe!"–only to go on doing all these abominations?
Jeremiah 7:8-10

Reflection

Dear Child of God, the Lord doesn't want us to deceive ourselves by thinking we can live in disobedience and hang on to His promises of protection and blessing. He doesn't want us to intentionally persist in sin and have false assurance in His mercy and promise of deliverance. To obtain the promises of God, we must first turn away from sin and seek to be faithful to His Word, then we can be covered by the promises of His protection and help.

PRAYER

Lord Jesus, open my eyes to see what you want me to do, what you want me to repent of and what may prevent me from the promise of your help.
Amen.

Day 20

I HAVE NOT COME TO CONDEMN YOU

*¹¹She said, "No one, sir." And Jesus
said, "Neither do I condemn you.
Go your way, and from now on do not
sin again."*
John 8:11

Reflection

Dear Child of God, Jesus has not come to condemn you or any one of us. He has come to reconcile us to one another and to the Father, to heal the wounds of sin and division, to set us free from the bondage of sin, to liberate us from the fear of death. Let us keep in mind that there is no condemnation for those in Christ Jesus. We are people who are set free. Let us not willingly surrender again to the power of sin which brings bondage and condemnation.

PRAYER

Lord Jesus, thank you for redeeming me from the bondage of sin and condemnation due to sin. Help me to live daily in the joy and freedom of being free to live for you.
Amen.

THOSE WHO ENDURED TO THE LAST

¹³ But the one who endures to the end
will be saved.
Matthew 24:13

Reflection

Dear Child of God, we may face the temptation of giving up on something good we have begun, something good that God has placed in our heart - a resolution, a mission, a salutary decision, a commendable project, a worthy plan, a noble vision. Keep in mind today that perseverance and determination are essential to achieve God's purpose and unless we persevere to the end, we may not be able to reach the joy of fulfilment and the salvation already won for us in Christ Jesus.

PRAYER

Lord Jesus, give me the strength to persevere in fulfilling your purpose. May I not give in to discouragement and despair.
Amen.

Day 22

HE HONOURED HIS NAME

*²I bow down toward your holy
temple and give thanks to your name for
your steadfast love and your faithfulness;
for you have exalted your name and
your Word above everything.*
Psalm 138:2

Reflection

God cares so much about the honour of His name and
His words. He wants us to hold His name holy, to
revere His holy name and to call upon it in prayer with
faith. Most importantly, we who are called by His
name must avoid anything that will bring dishonour to
that name.

PRAYER

Lord Jesus, I honour your name which is above
every name. May I constantly hold this name
with reverence and seek after all that does it
honour.
Amen.

Day 23

WISDOM PROVEN THROUGH GOOD LIFE

[13] Who is wise and understanding among you? Show by your good life that your works are done with gentleness born of wisdom.
James 3:13

Reflection

Dear Child of God, the Lord wants us to demonstrate that we are wise by living a good life. Wisdom from God doesn't consist in a life of jealousy, selfishness, arrogance, malice, grudge, sexual impurity, or uncontrolled anger. We reflect divine wisdom by gentleness, meekness, purity, openness to correction, truthfulness, kindness and mercy.

PRAYER

Lord Jesus, help me to live a good life, a life that clearly demonstrates the wisdom of the Holy Spirit.
Amen.

Day 24

APPRECIATE TODAY

*14 Yet you do not even know what
tomorrow will bring. What is your life?
For you are a mist that appears for a little
while and then vanishes. 15 Instead you
ought to say, "If the Lord wishes, we will
live and do this or that."*
James 4:14-15

Reflection

Dear Child of God, time is an important and invaluable gift of God to us. There is yesterday which has passed, there is tomorrow, which is yet to come and still unknown. We also have today which is the present moment we are living in. The Lord has given us today to do what is good and right and will bring us happiness tomorrow. Let us stop living in yesterday. Let us not waste our time today or presume about tomorrow because only God knows what tomorrow holds.

PRAYER

Lord Jesus, help me to spend my time today wisely, seeking what will bring me happiness tomorrow. Save me from wasting time or acting in a way that will bring me sadness and regret later.
Amen.

Day 25

CONTROL YOUR BODY IN NOMINEES AND HONOUR

³For this is the will of God, your sanctification: that you abstain from fornication; ⁴that each one of you know how to control your own body in holiness and honour, ⁵not with lustful passion, like the Gentiles who do not know God
1 Thessalonians 4:3-5

Reflection

Dear Child of God, your body is a temple of the Holy Spirit. It is sacred and it is to be offered to God as a sacrifice with a sweet fragrance. Avoid everything that can soil or contaminate that offering. Sexual impurity defiles our body and offends the holiness of God. Be careful to control your body in holiness and honour and not allow it to be used as an instrument of sin.

PRAYER

Lord Jesus, help me to shun anything that can defile my body. Help me to present my body to God as a sanctified temple fitting for the indwelling of His Holy Spirit.
Amen.

Day 26

WITH HIM ALL THINGS ARE POSSIBLE

[37] For nothing will be impossible with God.
Luke 1:37

Reflection

Dear Child of God, we should keep in mind today that with God no situation is hopeless, no condition is unchangeable, no enemy is unconquerable, no matter is irredeemable, no sinner cannot be restored, no sickness is incurable, no darkness cannot be dispelled. He is a miracle working God and His power is infinite. We should remind ourselves as many times as possible today that with Him, all things are possible.

PRAYER

Lord Jesus, may I ever keep in mind today and always that with you, nothing is impossible, for all things obey your will.
Amen.

Day 27

YOU ARE MINE

*⁴³ But now thus says the Lord, He who
created you, O Jacob, He who formed
you, O Israel: Do not fear, for I have
redeemed you; I have called you by
name, you are mine.*

Isaiah 43:1

Reflection

Dear Child of God, God is saying something so
important to us, and understanding this should fill us
with great joy and pride. God says each of us belongs
to Him. We may not be special in the eyes of the world,
we may be messed up in our own eyes, we may have
no form or comeliness for people to notice, adore or
celebrate us but God says we belong to Him. He loves
us, He claims us. We are not without an owner. God
says He claims ownership of us, and His stamp is on
us. We are possessions of an awesome God and as such
we are infinitely significant.

PRAYER

Lord Jesus, help me to keep in mind always that
I belong to God, that I am totally and
completely His and your blood is the ransom
paid for me.
Amen.

Day 28

DEATH IS GAIN

*²¹ For to me, living is Christ and
dying is gain.*
Philippians 1:21

Reflection

Death is something most of us dread. We don't want to think or talk about it. We fear the process of dying and the sadness of being separated from our loved ones. Today St. Paul reminds us that when we live for Christ, death is a great gain, and who we are going to see is more important than what we are leaving behind.

PRAYER

Lord Jesus, help me to live for you so that death may bring an end to the temptations and suffering of life and usher me into your glorious presence.
Amen.

EXAMINE YOUR INTENTION

*³ Do nothing from selfish ambition or
conceit, but in humility regard others as
better than yourselves.*
Philippians 2:3

Reflection

Dear Child of God, the Lord wants us to examine the motives behind our actions. Wrong intention may corrupt a good deed. Let us carefully purge out selfishness or pride from our actions and do all we are called to do with genuine charity, true humility and out of the desire to glorify God and Him alone.

PRAYER

Lord Jesus, help me to purge my deeds of all pride and selfishness. May I be always motivated by love of you and sincere love and respect for others.
Amen.

Day 30

GOD'S NAME

*⁷You shall not make wrongful use of the
name of the Lord your God, for
the Lord will not acquit anyone who
misuses His name.*
Exodus 20:7

Reflection

Dear Child of God, be careful to give honour to God's name. Do not invoke God's name in vain, and do not testify to what is not true. Be careful of calling on God in careless speech. Call on God's name with reverence as you pray and sing in honour of the glory of His name. There is power in the name of the Lord. To call on God's name is to invoke the presence and power of God Himself.

PRAYER

Lord Jesus, you teach us to hallow God's name.
Help me to avoid profaning the name which is
above every other name.
Amen.

Day 31
RELIGIOUS PURITY

*⁶ If any turn to mediums and wizards,
prostituting themselves to them, I will set
my face against them, and will cut them
off from the people.*
Leviticus 20:6

Reflection

Dear Child of God, it is a dishonour to God if we contaminate ourselves by engaging in pagan practices, by participating in activities and customs that do not confirm to our faith. Let us carefully resist all forms of paganism, idolatry or anything with such appearance. We belong to the kingdom of light, let us not be lured into practices that are opposed to true religion.

PRAYER

Lord Jesus, everything I need is in you. May I never turn to anything that is opposed to true worship of God.
Amen.

FEBRUARY

Day 1
RIGHT LIVING HONOURS GOD

*8 If the Lord is pleased with us, He will
bring us into this land and give it to us,
a land that flows with milk and honey.*
Numbers 14:8

Reflection

Dear Child of God, if the Lord wishes, there is nothing impossible for Him to do for us. He loves us despite our weakness and sinfulness, however our sin may obstruct the flow of His grace and blessing in our lives. The Lord delights in us as His children but our effort at living rightly gives Him great honour and opens the door of blessing for us.

PRAYER

Lord Jesus, help me to purge out of my life anything that you take no delight in.
Amen.

Day 2

GOD KNOWS THOSE WHO SERVE HIM

⁷ But not a dog shall growl at any of the Israelites—not at people, not at animals—so that you may know that the Lord makes a distinction between Egypt and Israel.
Exodus 11:7

Reflection

When the Lord sent the final plague on Egypt, the plague that compelled Pharaoh to set God's people free, God made provisions for His children to be protected from misfortune and death. He made a distinction between the Israelites and the Egyptians. Dear Child of God, in Christ we learn that God's love reaches all, both the good and the bad. However, God knows those whose hearts are with Him, those who are faithful to Him. He knows those who serve Him sincerely, and He makes the distinction between them and the hypocrites, the sheep and the goat. Where do we belong?

PRAYER

Lord Jesus, help me to be true and faithful to the Father and to be among those whose hearts are with Him.

Amen.

HAVE NO OTHER GOD

³you shall have no other gods before me.
Exodus 20:3

Reflection

Dear Child of God, the Lord wants us to love, serve and worship Him with all our attention, affection and devotion. He doesn't want us to allow our minds to be distracted from Him. In the world today, many things are calling for our attention and competing with total love of God. May we be careful not to allow anything to take first place, which is the place of God in our lives. No matter how important anything is to us, it must bow to the primacy and supremacy of God.

PRAYER

Lord Jesus, help me to place God first as the most important thing in my life. May I not give equal or greater affection than my God, who is my all, to any other person or thing.
Amen.

Day 4

YOU HAVE STAYED TOO LONG

⁶The Lord our God spoke to us at Horeb,
saying, "You have stayed long enough at
this mountain."
Deuteronomy 1:6

Reflection

The Lord told Moses and the people while in Horeb, "you have stayed long enough at this mountain; turn and continue your journey."

Dear Child of God, the Lord doesn't want us to remain on one spot in our spiritual life. He doesn't want us to be fixated or stagnant. He wants us to keep growing and progressing in our journey with Him. Maybe God is telling you that you are taking too much time to make a good decision, to execute what He has put in your mind to do, to take a step of faith. Don't stay too long pondering and being indecisive. There is time for everything: a time to ponder and a time to decide.

PRAYER

Lord Jesus Christ, help me to move on and keep advancing in my spiritual life and journey. May I not rest comfortably on one spot.
Amen.

EVEN NATURE OBEYS HIM

*⁴¹ And they were filled with great awe and
said to one another, "Who then is this, that
even the wind and the sea obey Him?"*
Mark 4:41

Reflection

Jesus commanded the wind to stop and the disciples
were filled with awe. They wondered at His power, as
even the wind and sea obeyed Him. Dear Child of
God, if forces of nature hear the Word of Jesus and
obey, why then do we rational beings, created in His
image and likeness, fail to obey Him? Why do we like
to act in defiance to His voice? Why do we prefer to be
wilful and to do things our own way? Like the wind
and the sea, when we obey the voice of Jesus, there will
always be peace and calmness in our hearts. It is in
obeying Him that we can reach our final destination.

PRAYER

Lord Jesus, the sea and wind obey you. Give me
a spirit of obedience and submission to your
Word.
Amen.

Day 6

WISDOM TO GOVERN

*⁹Give your servant therefore an
understanding mind to govern your people,
able to discern between good and evil; for
who can govern this your great people?"*
1 Kings 3:9

Reflection

Solomon asked God for the gift of understanding in
order to govern God's people and also for a discerning
spirit to differentiate between what is good and
evil. Sometimes we may encounter some difficult
people whom we find challenging and uneasy to relate
with, we encounter people with complex personalities
and temperaments whom we struggle to get along
with. Sometimes we encounter situations where we
really don't even know what is right and pleasing to the
Lord. Let us approach God daily for wisdom to deal
with difficult people and situations and most
importantly for the wisdom to govern our lives
according to right reason and God's will.

PRAYER

Lord Jesus, you are the wisdom of God
incarnate. Fill me with your Spirit of wisdom to
be able to relate well with others and guide my
life in accordance with God's will and pleasure.
Amen.

THE JOY OF THE LORD

*[10] Then he said to them, "Go your way, eat
the fat and drink sweet wine and send
portions of them to those for whom nothing
is prepared, for this day is holy to our Lord;
and do not be grieved, for the joy of
the Lord is your strength."*

Nehemiah 8:10

Reflection

There are times when we are really weighed down and
soul-distressed. There are times when tears just flow
freely from our eyes. There are times that we are really
broken and tired of it all. When our soul is downcast,
let us remember to turn to the Lord for comfort. Let
us ponder on God's love for us, His promises, His care
and the hope of salvation. When nothing gives us joy,
let us seek joy in the Lord. The awareness that He
holds us in His arms can dispel any sorrow, can revive
our bones and overwhelm us with joy. For the joy of
the Lord is our strength.

PRAYER

Lord Jesus, help me to find strength in the joy
that God gives through His love and care for
me.
Amen.

Day 8

GENEROSITY TO THE NEEDY

⁷give alms from your possessions, and do not let
your eye begrudge the gift when you make it. Do
not turn your face away from anyone who is poor,
and the face of God will not be turned away from
you. ⁸If you have many possessions, make your
gift from them in proportion; if few, do not be
afraid to give according to the little you have.

Tobit 4:7-8

Reflection

Tobit instructs his son to be generous and not be
unmoved by the needs of the poor around him. No
matter how little we have, we are encouraged to share
with the needy. The value of what is given is not
usually in the quantity but in the love in our heart, the
joy in our eyes and the noble intention driving us to do
it. When we are kind and generous to others, we do not
only show our love for them but also our gratitude to
God and we dispose ourselves to receive more from
Him. For whoever is generous to the needy will
experience God's gracious generosity.

PRAYER

Lord Jesus, help me to be kind and generous to
those in need. May I find joy and satisfaction in
coming to the aid of those in genuine need.
Amen.

THOSE WHO WAIT ON THE LORD

²⁴ Be strong, and let your heart take courage, all you who wait for the Lord.
Psalm 31:24

Reflection

Sometimes waiting for the Lord can be very difficult and challenging. Sometimes our heart begins to grow faint. We are tempted to give up, bow to despair or seek alternatives outside of what God permits.

Dear Child of God, are you waiting on God for anything? Keep in mind the words of the Psalmist - be strong, let your heart take courage, do not be swayed and do not waver in faith. Those who wait on the Lord shall not be put to shame.

PRAYER

Lord Jesus, give me the strength and courage to wait patiently for the fulfilment of all your promises in my life. You have shown me that you are trustworthy and so I hold firmly unto you.
Amen.

Day 10

LET YOUR YES BE YES

*¹²Above all, my beloved, do not swear,
either by heaven or by earth or by any other
oath, but let your "Yes" be yes and your
"No" be no, so that you may not fall under
condemnation.*
James 5:12

Reflection

Dear Child of God, our God is always truthful. In Him there is no deceit, no shadow of alteration, no inconsistency. As His children, He wants us to be trustworthy and truthful always. There is no need for us to swear to attest to anything. Let us say what is, that it is and to what is not, that it is not and not adopt the tactics of lying, even for a good end.

PRAYER

Lord Jesus, you are the truth. Help me to witness to you always and to desist from saying or promoting whatever is false.
Amen.

THE VIRTUOUS WILL SHINE

³Those who are wise shall shine like the brightness of the sky and those who lead many to righteousness, like the stars forever and ever.
Daniel 12:3

Reflection

Dear Child of God, it is displeasing to God that many of His children are ignorant of what He requires of them and that many are turning away from the path of righteousness. It is God's will and pleasure that we help others to discover and turn to the path of obedience to Him, that we act as the voice of truth to others. The Lord says those who help others to turn to the path of righteousness will shine like stars for all eternity.

PRAYER

Lord Jesus, I give myself to you to use as an instrument for helping others to know and love you and to abandon the path of error and damnation.
Amen.

Day 12
YOU ARE NOT A JUDGE

37 "Do not judge, and you will not be judged; do not condemn, and you will not be condemned. Forgive, and you will be forgiven
Luke 6:37

Reflection

Dear Child of God, the Lord does not want us to position ourselves as a judge of others. If we identify something wrong, we have an obligation to help the person concerned but this must be done in charity and humility. We must avoid condemning people because of their weaknesses and imperfections. We are all weak and struggling in one way or another. People often go through struggles that we are unaware of. Understanding this will help us to be more compassionate and forgiving.

PRAYER

Lord Jesus, you have not come to judge but to save sinners. Help me to refrain from being hasty and uncharitable in my assessment of people and their actions.
Amen.

Day 13

HE IS ABLE

²⁰ Now to Him who by the power at work within us is able to accomplish abundantly far more than all we can ask or imagine
Ephesians 3:20

Reflection

Dear Child of God, whenever we come before God, let us keep in mind that we are not coming before someone who is good but unable to help us as we desire, someone with a good will but lacking strength to bring about what He wills. St. Paul reminds us that He is able to do far more abundantly than we can ever ask or imagine, and His power is even at work within us. This means we are also able to do far more than we think or imagine. With this, let us approach God setting aside any minimalist mentality and approach life with the awareness of God's power within us.

PRAYER

Lord Jesus, I know you are able to do exceedingly more than I can ask or imagine. Help me to approach you with this awareness and assurance that you can and are willing to give even more than I can ask.
Amen.

Day 14

I WILL NOT FORSAKE YOU

⁶ Be strong and bold; have no fear or dread
of them, because it is the Lord your God
who goes with you; He will not fail you or
forsake you."
Deuteronomy 31:6

Reflection

Dear Child of God, what you are going through doesn't matter much when you realise who is there with you. The Lord says to you today, have courage, do not fear, be strong. He says He will go with you, He will not leave or forsake you. With this assurance, face your challenges with a good spirit. However, be careful not to go to where God doesn't want you to go; stay where His promises will cover you.

PRAYER

Lord Jesus, make me more aware of your loving presence. Give me courage and strength to face my challenges with a victorious spirit.
Amen.

47

Day 15

FOCUS ON JESUS

*² looking to Jesus the pioneer and perfecter
of our faith, who for the sake of the joy that
was set before Him endured the cross,
disregarding its shame, and has taken His
seat at the right hand of the throne of God.*
Hebrews 12:2

Reflection

Dear Child of God, we are reminded to focus on Jesus
- to focus on who He is and what He has done for us,
to focus on Him for strength, acceptance,
encouragement, for reward, inspiration and for
help. Often we focus on the wrong people and the
wrong things and so we are easily disturbed,
disappointed, misled and we are left broken. When we
focus on Jesus we receive the strength and grace to run
the race of life and run it well to a glorious end.

PRAYER

Lord Jesus, help me to focus on you and not on
the distractions around me.
Amen.

Day 16

WE SHALL RENDER AN ACCOUNT

[10] For all of us must appear before the judgment seat of Christ, so that each may receive recompense for what has been done in the body, whether good or evil.
2 Corinthians 5:10

Reflection

Dear Child of God, let us keep in mind that one day we shall all appear before the judgement seat of God, and we shall render account of our lives. Our concern should not just be whether we are seen or known by someone. Let us keep in mind that God sees and knows us and nothing about us is hidden. This all seeing, impartial judge will be our judge. This doesn't call for fear but for caution and wisdom. Let us desist from anything that will bring us shame when we stand before Him.

PRAYER

Lord Jesus, you are my saviour and my Lord, but you are also my just judge. Help me by your grace, to conduct my life so as to stand blameless before you on the day of judgement. Amen.

I WILL BE A FATHER TO YOU

*¹⁸ and I will be your father, and you shall be
my sons and daughters, says the Lord
Almighty."*
2 Corinthians 6:18

Reflection

Dear Child of God, the Lord is renewing His promise
to you today - He will be a Father to you. He will
protect you, provide for you and preserve you. He will
bring you to His side and lavish His love on you. He is
such a loving and caring Father. If He has promised to
be a Father to you, then you must also be willing to be
a good, obedient and responsible child to Him.

PRAYER

Lord Jesus, thank you for welcoming me to the
family of God's people. I rejoice in the honour of
my adoption. I pray for strength to be a good
child of God, one who will bring honour and not
disrepute to the name of his Father.
Amen.

Day 18

LAY ASIDE ENCUMBRANCES

*12 Therefore, since we are surrounded by so
great a cloud of witnesses, let us also lay
aside every weight and the sin that clings so
closely, and let us run with perseverance the
race that is set before us*
Hebrews 12:1

Reflection

Dear Child of God, life is a race. We are running towards the prize which Christ has won for us. The journey is long and tough, but God's grace has been provided in abundant measure. Let us therefore run with perseverance. Let us lay aside whatever will make it difficult for us to win the crown of glory awaiting us. The road is narrow and so whoever travels it must travel light. Sin takes us through the wrong road and love of the world makes the journey difficult.

PRAYER

Lord Jesus, help me to lay aside whatever will be an obstruction in my journey towards you, you who are the fulfilment of all my desires and joys.
Amen.

Day 19

WE WALK BY FAITH

⁷for we walk by faith, not by sight.
2 Corinthians 5:7

Reflection

Dear Child of God, there is more to life and reality than what we can see. Faith gives us a clearer picture of reality and takes us beyond what the physical eye can see. Faith is seeing with our inner eye. Faith is trusting in what God has said and done, even though our human senses can't comprehend it. Faith helps us to make sense of life and to keep walking, even in the midst of thick darkness and bottomless uncertainty. Life without faith is dark and dreary. Therefore let us hold unto our faith and when our senses fail us, we can keep walking on until we reach our desired haven.

PRAYER

Lord Jesus, I surrender in faith to you. I believe all that you have said and promised because in you there is no deceit and when I walk with you in faith, I walk secure.
Amen.

Day 20

REJOICE IN THE LORD

4 Rejoice in the Lord always; again I will say, Rejoice.
Philippians 4:4

Reflection

There are so many things in our world today that threaten one's joy. A logical assessment of events in the world is enough to break someone. It is not a surprise that many people are relapsing into depression and pessimism. O Child of God, the Lord wants us to rejoice. He wants us to rejoice that He is our Father, that He knows us, and that He won't forsake or forget us. We should rejoice in the joy of our salvation, rejoice in the hope that when this earthly dwelling is destroyed, we have the hope of a glorious home in the company of God's holy angels and saints. In this hope, the Lord wants us to rejoice.

PRAYER

Lord Jesus, thank you for giving me reasons to be joyful. May nothing take away my joy in you.
Amen.

COURTESY TOWARDS ALL PEOPLE

²to speak evil of no one, to avoid quarrelling, to be gentle, and to show every courtesy to everyone.

Titus 3:2

Reflection

Dear Child of God, the Lord wants you to speak charitably of people. There is something good in everyone, no matter how bad they seem. The Lord wants you to show courtesy towards all people, irrespective of their status. The Lord wants you to avoid quarrelling as much as possible. These are the ways that we witness to the world that the Spirit of Christ is in us.

PRAYER

Lord Jesus, help me to be watchful of my words and my ways today. May you be in my words, thoughts and actions, today and always. Amen.

Day 22

LEAD BY EXAMPLE

*³ Remind them to be subject to rulers and
authorities, to be obedient,
to be ready for every good work*
Titus 3:1

Reflection

Dear Child of God, keep in mind that you must lead by good example wherever you are. Be first to obey just laws and submit to legitimate authorities in what doesn't violate your conscience and faith. We cannot be good Christians if we are not first good citizens. Let us show the world how to make the world a better place through obedience and universal fraternity.

PRAYER

Lord Jesus, help me to be obedient and submissive to authorities, and strengthen my resolve to be law-abiding and respectful of all you have made.
Amen.

A MODEL OF GOOD DEEDS

7 For a bishop, as God's steward, must be blameless; he must not be arrogant or quick-tempered or addicted to wine or violent or greedy for gain
Titus 1:7

Reflection

Dear Child of God, show yourself in all respects as a model of good deeds. Wherever you are, in any organisation you work, amongst your colleagues and friends, be a blessing, an inspiration, a teacher of how to live a good life. People say fine things about the deceased; live in a way that the good testimonies of people about you when you are no more, will not be untrue or an exaggeration.

PRAYER

Lord Jesus, help me to be a model of good deeds. Help me to cooperate with your grace in order to be kind, loving and fair to everyone. Amen.

Day 24

WALKING IN FAITH AND OBEDIENCE

¹⁷*The Lord said to Moses, "I will do the very thing that you have asked; for you have found favour in my sight, and I know you by name."*
Exodus 33:17

Reflection

The Lord promised to fulfil the wish of Moses because He had found favour in God's sight. Moses walked in faith and obedience with God. He did his best to please God even though he had his personal weaknesses and struggles, and God loved Him and honoured His words. God loves and honours every one of us, not precisely because of our innate goodness but because of the righteousness of Christ which is on us. However, God is impressed when we are committed to Him like Moses and we walk faithfully in His way, and He does great things through us and for others.

PRAYER

Lord Jesus, help me to walk faithfully with you. Help me to honour you by my entire life. May I find favour in your sight and may you be attentive to the voice of my prayers.
Amen.

Day 25

FULFIL YOUR VOWS TO THE LORD

*2 When a man makes a vow to the Lord or
swears an oath to bind himself by a pledge, he
shall not break his word; he shall do according
to all that proceeds out of his mouth.*
Numbers 30:2

Reflection

Dear Child of God, have you promised anything to
God? Have you said anything in God's presence? Have
you made any vow to the Lord or in the assembly of
His faithful? These are not empty words. Whatever
you have promised or vowed to the Lord is binding.
Make efforts to be faithful and to fulfil whatever you
have said before the Lord. Sometimes it is difficult,
especially when circumstances threaten our will,
however, if you are firm in purpose and rely on God's
strength, He will help and support you to fulfil
everything that you have promised.

PRAYER

Lord Jesus, at baptism, I promised to renounce
Satan, all his works and empty promises. Help
me to remain faithful to my promises and never
be found wanting in my vows to you.
Amen.

Day 26

JONATHAN, A TRUE FRIEND

17 Jonathan made David swear again by his love for him; for he loved him as he loved his own life.
1 Samuel 20:17

Reflection

Jonathan is an example of true love and friendship. Even though his father Saul tried to instigate him to hate David for no just cause, he continued to love him and was faithful to him. He protected David and was very kind to him. He ensured no harm came upon David even though he knew that David was a threat to his ascent to his father's throne. Jonathan is an example of a true, selfless and faithful friend. Friends like this are scarce in our world today. There is so much betrayal, self-centredness and malice among friends today. As we complain that good friends are scarce, let us try to be one, and let us try to make people's lives better by our presence in them.

PRAYER

Lord Jesus, help me to be a good friend, loving others as I want to be loved and as you love me. Amen.

Day 27

IT'S TIME TO BE GRATEFUL

*¹⁸ Then King David went in and sat before
the Lord, and said, "Who am I, O
Lord God, and what is my house, that you
have brought me thus far?*
2 Samuel 7:18

Reflection

When King David heard of God's plan for him, as announced through the prophet Nathan, he sat before the Lord and marvelled at what God had promised and why God had promised such incomprehensibly massive blessings to him. He said, *who am I, O Lord God, and what is my house, that you have brought me thus far?* Dear Child of God, think of who you were, ponder on how far God has brought you, spend time in His presence just to be grateful. If you examine your journey of life carefully, you will see that God has been very good to you.

PRAYER

Lord Jesus, thank you for bringing me thus far. I trust you to perfect your work in me and bring me safely home.
Amen.

Day 28

HE A MERCIFUL GOD

5 "Turn back, and say to Hezekiah prince of my people, Thus says the Lord, the God of your ancestor David: I have heard your prayer, I have seen your tears; indeed, I will heal you; on the third day you shall go up to the house of the Lord."
2 Kings 20:5

Reflection

Hezekiah received a message that he would die. He cried to the Lord, he prayed earnestly and asked for mercy. God sent the prophet Isaiah back to him, to tell him that He had considered him and that He would show him mercy. Dear Child of God, do not say, "in vain have I cried and called on the Lord." We do not serve a God who is unmoved by prayers or who is indifferent to our cries. He is a merciful and compassionate God who listens to our prayers. As you call on him today, be assured that He is not indifferent or aloof. He hears and He will give to you what is best for you, in His way, at the best time.

PRAYER

Lord Jesus, as I call upon you, may I be reassured that my prayers and supplications are not made in vain and that in your name I will receive more than I dare to ask.
Amen.

(For A Leap Year)

GIVE THANKS IN ALL CIRCUMSTANCES

*18 give thanks in all circumstances; for this
is the will of God in Christ Jesus for you.*
1 Thessalonians 5:18

Reflection

There are times when we don't really feel like giving thanks. There are times when we are just worried, unhappy and disturbed. Dear Child of God, the Lord wants you to give thanks in all circumstances. This means giving thanks not by feeling, but as a decision we must make. When we give thanks, we trust God to take care of our situation, we confess God's goodness. Every act of thanksgiving begets more reasons for thanksgiving. When we give thanks where the devil expects us to cry in bitter lamentation, we put the devil to shame and we glorify God. In that condition, God moves in our favour.

PRAYER

Lord Jesus, teach me to see your goodness in everything and may I never stop singing your praises.
Amen.

MARCH

THOSE WHO WAIT ON THE LORD

³¹ but those who wait for the LORD shall renew their strength, they shall mount up with wings like eagles, they shall run and not be weary, they shall walk and not faint.
Isaiah 40:31

Reflection

God gives strength to those who rely on Him, those who place their hope in Him and look to Him for the satisfaction of their desires. They will not be wearied, they will not be exhausted because of the stress of life. The Lord promises to supply them with inner strength to soar above everything else - the strength to run and walk. They will march forward and make progress in their life journey. Dear Child of God, if we are getting weak because of the stress of life, we should call on the Lord for strength and we will be renewed and revived.

PRAYER

Lord Jesus, I look to you for help. When I am weak, give me the strength to carry on in my journey of faith.
Amen.

Day 2

STAND FIRM IN YOUR FAITH

---

¹³ Keep alert, stand firm in your faith, be courageous, be strong.
1 Corinthians 16:13

Reflection

St. Paul reminds us to keep alert, to be very careful and discerning, to be firm and convinced. This is because there is so much in the world today that can confuse us and rob us of our faith and hope in Christ. Dear Child of God, there is so much deception and confusion in our world. Know your faith and carefully refute deceitful arguments and pretentious teachings that are damaging to the purity of faith. We must keep alert so that no one robs us of our faith, the knowledge of the truth and our peace in Christ Jesus.

PRAYER

Lord Jesus, help me to keep alert and resist everything that might pose danger to my faith and love for you.
Amen.

THE SUPREMACY OF LOVING THE HUMAN PERSON

10 Then the LORD said, "You are concerned about the bush, for which you did not labour and which you did not grow; it came into being in a night and perished in a night. 11 And should I not be concerned about Nineveh, that great city, in which there are more than a hundred and twenty thousand persons who do not know their right hand from their left, and also many animals?"

Jonah 4:10-11

Reflection

Jonah was very angry that the tree which gave him shade was allowed to wither but then he wanted the whole of Nineveh to perish. Dear Child of God, the souls of people are more important than things. All that God has created is important to God, but He has given first place to the human person. Let us not allow love of other created things to supersede the love of our brethren. Let us not be protective of things over people. Let us not rejoice or pray that any of God's creatures should perish or suffer harm.

PRAYER

Lord Jesus, help me to recognise that placing a priority on the things of this world over people is not following your way. Let me love my neighbour, mirroring the love you show all people.
Amen.

Day 4

NO GREATER LOVE

*¹³ No one has greater love than this, to lay
down one's life for one's friends.*
John 15:13

Reflection

The love of Jesus for us is great and immeasurable. He
gave everything for us including His life. What manner
of love is this? Dear Child of God, each time we look
at the crucifix, let us ponder on the love of Jesus for us,
how He suffered and died for us even when we were
still sinners and undeserving. This is a love so amazing
and so divine. Let the thought of this love prompt us
to ask, "how can I repay the Lord for His love for me?"

PRAYER

Lord Jesus, your love for me surpasses my
imagination and understanding. Help me to
reciprocate that love by loving you beyond
everything, even my life.
Amen.

Day 5

SUCCESS IN OBEDIENCE

*7 Only be strong and very courageous, being
careful to act in accordance with all the law
that my servant Moses commanded you; do not
turn from it to the right hand or to the left, so
that you may be successful wherever you go.*
Joshua 1:7

Reflection

Joshua was told the secret of success - unwavering
obedience to the commands of God. His heart must be
with the Lord and not be distracted, he should not turn
to the right or left to copy the sinful practices of nations
around him. Dear Child of God, obedience to the Lord
brings blessing to us. Let us not be distracted or misled
by the sinful influence and corrupt examples of people
but remain focused on following the Lord on the path
of obedience and faithfulness. In this lies the secret of
success.

PRAYER
Lord Jesus, help me to follow you in obedience
and not to allow myself to be lured into
whatever offends your holiness and love for me.
Amen.

Day 6

ALL THINGS ARE WORKING FOR GOOD

28 We know that all things work together for good for those who love God, who are called according to His purpose.
Romans 8:28

Reflection

Dear Child of God, here is a great reminder that all things are ordered for our good. All things are made to serve God's purpose in our lives. Once there is love of God in us and we learn to place our trust in God, we need not worry ourselves about the turn of events because it shall eventually be in our favour. God works through everything around us to favour and bless us. Let this be our confession and it will also be our testimony.

PRAYER

Lord Jesus, I confess and declare that I am sure that all things are working for my good, even though I may not understand your ways and it may not appear so.
Amen.

Day 7

YET, I WILL REJOICE

*¹⁷ Though the fig tree does not blossom, and no fruit
is on the vines; though the produce of the olive fails,
and the fields yield no food; though the flock is cut off
from the fold, and there is no herd in the stalls, ¹⁸ yet
I will rejoice in the LORD I will exult in the God of
my salvation.*

Habakkuk 3:17-18

Reflection

The prophet Habakkuk confessed that nothing would
stop him from rejoicing in the Lord. He would rejoice
in abundance or scarcity. He would rejoice whether
times look favourable or otherwise. He would rejoice
and praise the Lord in season and out of season. Dear
Child of God, God is looking for people who will
praise and rejoice in Him no matter the condition. He
is looking for those who recognise His goodness in fair
season and in stormy weather. To be able to praise God
even when the sun goes down is evidence of deep faith
and such worship is powerful and efficacious.

PRAYER

Lord Jesus, may nothing stop me from praising
you. In scarcity or abundance, in sickness or
health, may my soul never stop magnifying
you.

Amen.

Day 8

To Find Jesus Is To Find Everything

⁷ Yet whatever gains I had, these I have come to regard as loss because of Christ.
Philippians 3:7

Reflection

St. Paul had great advantages and privileges. However, he confessed that his enviable human achievements paled before his new achievement which was finding Christ Jesus or being found by Christ. To find Jesus is to have everything. There is so much joy in the Lord, more than all the world's success and achievements can ever afford. Dear Child of God, we must not seek so much joy in the passing things of this world. We must seek to know the Lord more and ask for an experience of the power of His love. We will experience something of the joy of heaven in our soul, and there will be no gain greater than this.

PRAYER

Lord Jesus, give me a thirst for you with every passing day, that I may come to know you better. Draw me nearer to you Lord and keep me moment by moment wrapped in your grace and love.
Amen.

EVEN THOUGH I WALK THROUGH

*⁴ Even though I walk through the darkest
valley, I fear no evil; for you are with me; your
rod and your staff–they comfort me.*
Psalm 23:4

Reflection

The Psalmist sings of walking through the darkest valley. Dear Child of God, when we feel like someone in a dark valley, a bleak tunnel, a seemingly endless cycle of misfortune, we should keep in mind two things. We are not alone, and we are only walking through. God is there with us, and we should allow Him to comfort us and not believe that this is our habitation. We are only walking through the dark tunnel, and we will soon be ushered into the brightness of glory, if we do not faint, lose heart or lose sight of the one who promises us comfort.

PRAYER

Lord Jesus, I trust in you as I walk through the dark valley. Hold my hands and lead me into the glorious future ahead of me.
Amen.

72

Day 10

SEEK FIRST

³³ But strive first for the kingdom of God and His righteousness, and all these things will be given to you as well.
Matthew 6:33

Reflection

There are so many things calling for our attention in this world, so many things we want to achieve and possess, so many things in life we want to grasp and fit into our backpack. Dear Child of God, the Lord tells us to pause and set our priorities right. We should seek what is most important and let the rest come to us and if it doesn't, if we seek and gain heaven, we will never mourn the loss of anything. Heaven is our final goal and must be the greatest longing of every pilgrim soul.

PRAYER

Lord Jesus, help me to seek eternal life more than I seek anything else in this world.
Amen.

GOD WILL PROVIDE

⁸ Abraham said, "God himself will provide the lamb for a burnt offering, my son." So the two of them walked on together.
Genesis 22:8

Reflection

In obedience to God, Abraham took his only son Isaac to be offered in sacrifice. On the way, the son asked "Father, where is the lamb of sacrifice?" Abraham in faith replied to him, "the Lord will provide" and the Lord indeed provided.

Dear Child of God, the Lord is a great provider. Let us trust Him to provide what we need for our spiritual, physical, mental and social wellbeing. When we are in any form of need, confess like Abraham. I know the Lord knows my need and in His own way, He will provide.

PRAYER

Lord Jesus, help me to trust that you know my need and you will not allow me to lack whatever is necessary for my wellbeing.
Amen.

Day 12

CHRIST HAS SET YOU FREE

1 For freedom Christ has set us free. Stand firm, therefore, and do not submit again to a yoke of slavery.
Galatians 5:1

Reflection

In Christ Jesus, we have freedom from the greatest form of slavery - slavery under sin and the flesh. The blood of Jesus has set us free. We have been set free to live a new life, not according to the instinct of sin but according to the principles of the Word of God. Dear Child of God, let us be careful therefore not to surrender ourselves into the slavery of sin anymore. When we plunge ourselves back into the habit of sin, we surrender to slavery and we lose our spiritual liberty.

PRAYER

Lord Jesus, thank you for setting me free. May I never again surrender myself to sin.
Amen.

POSITIVE SPIRIT

*30 But Caleb quieted the people before Moses,
and said, "Let us go up at once and occupy it,
for we are well able to overcome it."*
Numbers 13:30

Reflection

The people of Israel who were sent to spy on the land of Canaan came back with a very good report about the land but a terrible report about themselves. "The land is good and beautiful, but we are powerless and unable to possess it." Caleb quieted them and reminded them that if the Lord had promised them the land then nothing would stop them from possessing it. Dear Child of God, like Caleb, we should approach every situation with a positive spirit. We should see God in every situation, bring Him into the picture and assure ourselves that we are well able to do what God wants us to do and to succeed in what God has prompted us to embark on.

PRAYER

Lord Jesus, I confess that I am able, blessed and I can do what you say I can do because I am who you say I am.
Amen.

Day 14

PUT TO DEATH

*⁵ Put to death, therefore, whatever in you is earthly:
fornication, impurity, passion, evil desire, and greed
(which is idolatry). ⁶ On account of these the wrath
of God is coming on those who are disobedient. ⁷
These are the ways you also once followed, when you
were living that life. ⁸ But now you must get rid of all
such things—anger, wrath, malice, slander, and
abusive language from your mouth.*
Colossians 3:5-8

Reflection

St. Paul reminds us that we must put to death whatever
is earthly in us, anything that can attract the displeasure
of God. We must not give permission to sin to possess
any of our faculties or senses. Dear Child of God, the
Lord your God wants us to remove from our system
every turmoil of fornication, impurity, passion, evil
desire, greed, anger, wrath, malice, slander and abusive
language. We must remove all this and put them to
death and fill those spaces with godly character and
pleasure.

PRAYER

Lord Jesus, I come to you today, I surrender to
your healing procedure. Scan me through and
remove everything growing in me that can
damage my spiritual health.
Amen.

Day 15

NO ROOM FOR VENGEANCE

18 You shall not take vengeance or bear a grudge against any of your people, but you shall love your neighbour as yourself: I am the LORD.
Leviticus 19:18

Reflection

Sometimes we feel the best way to respond to an offence is to exact vengeance. We can be so hurt by people that we begin to bear a grudge against them. Dear Child of God, the Lord says this to you today: do not take vengeance or bear a grudge against any of your people. Let us not allow the action of anyone to disrupt the love that is within us.

PRAYER

Lord Jesus, I bring before you the pains I feel as a result of those who have hurt me. Instead of retaliation, I submit to you to heal me and to help me to move on without resentment.
Amen.

Day 16

BE A SHINING EXAMPLE

*[14] Do all things without murmuring and
arguing, [15] so that you may be blameless and
innocent, children of God without blemish in
the midst of a crooked and perverse generation,
in which you shine like stars in the world.*
Philippians 2:14-15

Reflection

People are quick to argue and complain even when it is unnecessary. Many people are suspicious of authorities and they bear within them a rebellion spirit. O Child of God, we should be slow to complain or argue about anything. We should do what we have to do with joy and enthusiasm. Let our spirit of commitment and dedication be a shining example to people in the world. Let us keep ourselves incorrupt by the sinful influence around and seek to overcome what is wrong by our commitment to what is right.

PRAYER

Lord Jesus, help me to carry out what is justly expected of me with enthusiasm and in good spirit so that I may excel in all I undertake.
Amen.

Day 17

THE FAITHFULNESS OF RUTH

16 But Ruth said, "Do not press me to leave you or to turn back from following you! Where you go, I will go; where you lodge, I will lodge; your people shall be my people, and your God my God.
Ruth 1:16

Reflection

Naomi, the mother in law, wanted her daughters in law, Oprah and Ruth, to leave her and start their own lives since she had lost her two sons and was set to return to her hometown of Moab. Oprah kissed her goodbye, but Ruth clung to her. She would not leave her to be on her own. She wanted to be there for her. Naomi had been a kind mother in law to them, and when she needed support, Ruth chose to be there for her as well. Dear Child of God, remember that our kindness to others is like seed sowing. We will reap kindness as well. Like Ruth, we must try not to abandon people in their moments of need.

PRAYER

Lord Jesus, you have been there for me in my moment of need. May abundance and privileges not lure me away from you and from others who have helped me in my low moments.
Amen.

Day 18

BE AN AMBASSADOR
OF PEACE

⁵ Whatever house you enter, first say,
'Peace to this house!'
Luke 10:5

Reflection

Dear Child of God, the Lord wishes that we are all ambassadors of peace. He says in whatever house we enter, we should announce peace. Let our presence anywhere promote peace and harmony. Let people know us as people of peace, lovers of peace, preachers of peace and agents of peace. If our master is the Prince of Peace, then we ought to be a channel of peace. We must never be a trouble starter or the cause of strife among people but always be a bridge reconciling people.

PRAYER

Lord Jesus, make me an instrument of your peace. Where there is hatred, may I sow love. Where there is division, may I sow unity. Amen.

Day 19

MINISTERING TO CHILDREN

¹³ People were bringing little children to Him in order
that He might touch them; and the disciples spoke
sternly to them. ¹⁴ But when Jesus saw this, He was
indignant and said to them, "Let the little children
come to me; do not stop them; for it is to such as
these that the kingdom of God belongs.
Mark 10:13-14

Reflection

Children occupy a very special place in the heart of
Jesus. He loves them and cares about their growth. He
wants us to introduce little children to Him, so that
they grow in His love. It saddens the heart of the Lord
whenever we mislead or corrupt the innocent heart of
a child. The Lord is displeased when we neglect to
bring them up in the knowledge of faith. Dear Child
of God, anyone who commits him/herself to ensuring
the growth of faith in children, anyone who leads them
to Jesus by word and example, their guardian angel will
love and pray for such person. May we discover in this
a laudable vocation - the vocation of helping children
to come to Jesus.

PRAYER

Lord Jesus, you love little children. May I bring
as many as possible to you. Give me also a
childlike spirit with all the trust and innocence.
Amen.

Day 20
IF GOD IS FOR US

³¹ What then are we to say about these things?
If God is for us, who is against us?
Romans 8:31

Reflection

Dear Child of God, if the Lord is for you, then you need not fear the number of those against you because it matters not. What is important is that God is on your side. One with God is a majority. Even if everyone stands against you, you have no need to fear, worry or fret. When you are on the side of God, you are on the winning side.

PRAYER

Lord Jesus, I know that if you are on my side, it matters not who is against me. Help me to keep this in mind and to overcome any threat on me as a result of my loyalty to you.
Amen.

Day 21

THEY ARE NEW EVERY MORNING

*²² The steadfast love of the LORD never ceases,
His mercies never come to an end; ²³ they are
new every morning; great is your faithfulness.*
Lamentations 3:22-23

Reflection

Often people tend to think that God doesn't love them anymore; that He loved them when they were innocent, and He has withdrawn His love because of their mistakes and sins. Dear Child of God, nothing can stop God from loving you and His faithfulness never comes to an end. We do not gain His love by our personal merit. If we have His love, it is by the merit of Christ. Let this fill us with holy joy because the love of the Lord for us can never come to an end and His ocean of mercy cannot be drained.

PRAYER

Lord Jesus, thank you for your overwhelming love and mercy. May I never take these for granted.
Amen.

Day 22

ETERNAL WEIGHT OF GLORY

17 For this slight momentary affliction is preparing us for an eternal weight of glory beyond all measure.
2 Corinthians 4:17

Reflection

In this life, we have to go through some moments of tests, persecution and hardship. However, this is preparing us for an eternal weight of glory beyond all measure. Dear Child of God, let us keep in mind that what we go through can never be compared to what we are going to. With the joy of what lays ahead of us, let us carry our rugged cross knowing full well that one day we shall exchange it for a crown.

PRAYER

Lord Jesus, whatever I am facing in this life, let me remain steadfast in faith and moving towards a life of eternal happiness with you. Amen.

DO NOT RELY ON YOUR INSIGHT

⌒⊰⊱⌒

⁵ Trust in the LORD with all your heart, and do not rely on your own insight. ⁶ In all your ways acknowledge Him, and He will make straight your paths.
Proverbs 3:5-6

Reflection

O Child of God, one of the temptations we need to battle against is that of relying on our wisdom, knowledge, strength, power or achievement. All of these can fail and indeed they do fail. They are all fallible, temporal and unreliable. Let our trust be supremely in the Lord, relying on Him rather than on anything or anyone else, acknowledging Him as our source of strength and the cause of our success in life.

PRAYER

Lord Jesus, I do not trust anything that is exclusively mine, but I trust everything that is yours in me. May I not fail or falter as I place my hope in you.
Amen.

Day 24

IMPOSSIBLE TO PLEASE GOD WITHOUT FAITH

⁶And without faith it is impossible to please God, for whoever would approach Him must believe that He exists and that He rewards those who seek Him.
Hebrews 11:6

Reflection

Often people pray to God but still wonder if He is true, present and listening. People pray and doubt if it's the sensible thing to do. Many talk to God but are not convinced of His presence and power to help them. Dear Child of God, let nothing shake our faith. God is real, He hears our prayers, He sees our hidden tears. He is not an idea, concept or hallucination. He is the Lord of all and the rewarder of all who seek Him. With this conviction, we should approach God in faith and confidence.

PRAYER

Lord Jesus, I firmly believe in you and all you have taught about the Father. May I grow in the faith that He is near to me and He rewards those who seek Him diligently.
Amen.

HIS ANGER IS FOR A MOMENT

*⁵For His anger is but for a moment; His favour
is for a lifetime. Weeping may linger for the
night, but joy comes with the morning.*
Psalm 30:5

Reflection

No matter what we have done to God, He won't be angry with us forever. The moment we become aware of our offences and we truly repent of them, the Father embraces us. God's anger is unlike ours. Often we get angry and lose control and go outside the limit of sense. God's anger is more with the act than the actor. Dear Child of God, because God is loving and patient, He is always eager to pardon us and turn our mourning into rejoicing. Let us declare upon ourselves that our weeping may linger through the night, but our joy shall arrive with the dawn.

PRAYER

Lord Jesus, may I never cause you to be angry with me, but if I do, may I recognise it, repent and seek your pardon.
Amen.

Day 26
YOU ARE A CHILD OF GOD

¹ See what love the Father has given us, that we
should be called children of God; and that is
what we are. The reason the world does not
know us is that it did not know Him.
1 John 3:1

Reflection

Dear Child of God, think for a moment who we are –
we are children of God. Imagine this great love that
God has lavished on us. He calls us His children. The
creator and ruler of the universe has adopted us as His
sons and daughters. We are members of the most royal
family; we are heirs of the kingdom; we are siblings of
the angels and saints. We are extraordinary.

PRAYER

Lord Jesus, thank you for being my King and my
brother. May I not soil or stain this dignity but
live my life in a manner befitting of a noble child
of a royal family.
Amen.

AVOID HATRED

> *⁴ But when his brothers saw that their father loved him more than all his brothers, they hated him, and could not speak peaceably to him.*
> **Genesis 37:4**

Reflection

The brothers of Joseph hated him because his father loved him. This is an instance of someone's favour attracting the hostility of others. Dear Child of God, we must not hate anyone for any reason. We must not be angry with anyone because of their blessings or the favour they have received. Our envy and hatred do not serve God's purpose but make us malleable to be used by the evil one.

PRAYER

Lord Jesus, as I celebrate your grace in my life, I celebrate your grace in the lives of others too. Please keep my heart from envy and hatred. Amen.

Day 28

YOU ARE NOT IN THE DARKNESS

❦

⁴ But you, beloved, are not in darkness, for that day to surprise you like a thief.
1 Thessalonians 5:4

Reflection

Dear Child of God, Christ has called us out of darkness into His own wonderful light. Let us therefore not live as people in darkness. Let us live in the light of God's knowledge, in the light of righteousness, in the light of love. Anyone who lives in ignorance of God's word and His ways, lives in darkness; anyone who delights in sinful pleasure, lives in the darkness, and anyone who doesn't love exists in darkness.

PRAYER

Lord Jesus, dispel every darkness from my life. May I live always in the light of truth, love and holiness.
Amen.

Day 29

HE WILL BRING IT TO COMPLETION

*⁶ I am confident of this, that the one who began
a good work among you will bring it to
completion by the day of Jesus Christ.*
Philippians 1:6

Reflection

Dear Child of God, we should not be anxious or disturbed by whatever God has begun in us because He will bring it to a worthy fulfilment. God doesn't abandon any project. His works in our lives shall be brought to an amazing completion. His promise and purpose shall be incredibly fulfilled, and we will not be unfinished projects. He will perfect in time and eternity what He has begun in us.

PRAYER

Lord Jesus, help me to live in the confidence that what you have begun in me shall be completed graciously by you.
Amen.

Day 30

BE OPEN TO GOOD COUNSEL

²⁴ So Moses listened to his father-in-law and did all that he had said.
Exodus 18:24

Reflection

Moses was a man whom God spoke to. He enjoyed a unique and unprecedented intimate relationship with God, second only to that of Jesus Himself. As holy as Moses was, he was humble enough to listen to his father in law who advised him on how best to judge God's people without wearing himself out. He adopted this suggestion and it worked perfectly for him and for the people. Dear Child of God, let us never feel we are too knowledgeable to listen to anyone. Humility increases knowledge and it is an evidence of wisdom. Anyone who is always right in his/her own eyes cannot drink well from the well spring of wisdom outside of him/herself.

PRAYER

Lord Jesus, help me to be meek enough to accept good advice from others. Grant me also, the discernment to know and apply only what is right and pleasing to you.
Amen.

Day 31

ASK IN FAITH

[21] Jesus answered them, "Truly I tell you, if you have faith and do not doubt, not only will you do what has been done to the fig tree, but even if you say to this mountain, 'Be lifted up and thrown into the sea,' it will be done. [22] Whatever you ask for in prayer with faith, you will receive."
Matthew 21:21-22

Reflection

Faith is power. Jesus tells us today that whatever we ask for in prayer with faith, we shall receive. The key words are prayers and faith. Dear Child of God, prayer is the ordinary means of presenting our needs to the Lord, and faith is what gives force to our prayers. Faith is the conviction that the Lord hears us, and He is willing and able to help us. When we pray with this conviction, God hears us, and He gives us what is best for us according to His supreme wisdom and providence.

PRAYER

Lord Jesus, instil in me the love for prayers and bless me with the gift of faith, so that when I pray with faith, I may rejoice in the hope that I have been heard.
Amen.

APRIL

NOTHING CAN SEPARATE US FROM HIS LOVE

³⁸ For I am convinced that neither death, nor life, nor angels, nor rulers, nor things present, nor things to come, nor powers, ³⁹ nor height, nor depth, nor anything else in all creation, will be able to separate us from the love of God in Christ Jesus our Lord.

Romans 8:38-39

Reflection

Dear Child of God, let us not listen to the lie of the evil one who says God doesn't love us or He has stopped loving you. Nothing can separate us from God's love. He loves us through everything. On our own part too, let us not allow anything in this life to erode the love of God from our hearts. St. Augustine of Hippo says, "To fall in love with God is the greatest romance; to seek Him is the greatest adventure; to find Him, the greatest human achievement."

PRAYER

Lord Jesus, may I love you with all that is within me and may nothing separate me from your love in time and in eternity.
Amen.

Day 2

CHRISTIANS ARE TO BE CHEERFUL

²² A cheerful heart is a good medicine, but a downcast spirit dries up the bones.
Proverbs 17:22

Reflection

Redeemed Christians are meant to be joyful. A heart that has welcomed Christ ought to be cheerful. The presence of Christ in a heart ushers in a new dawn of joy. This joy within should shine in our faces rather than us sport sad, pessimistic looks.

Pope Francis said, "although the root of Christian joy lies in the fact that Christians are forgiven and redeemed, it can be perceived by others only through joyful behaviour. If you have the face of a funeral wake, how can they believe that you are redeemed, that your sins have been forgiven?"

Dear Child of God, do not suppress your joy, if you are happy in the Lord, tell your face.

PRAYER

Lord Jesus, thank you for giving me joy. Help me to show it in my countenance, words and actions.
Amen.

BE ROOTED IN LOVE

¹⁷ And that Christ may dwell in your hearts through faith, as you are being rooted and grounded in love.
Ephesians 3:17

Reflection

St. Paul prayed that Christ may dwell in their hearts through faith and that they may be rooted and grounded in love. When we are rooted and grounded in love, we are rooted and grounded in God - for God is love. Where there is love, there is God -love that is true, genuine, sacrificial, purged of all lust, selfishness and pretence. Dear Child of God, this is the kind of love that purifies the heart. This is the kind of love that can heal the world. This is the love the Lord wants us to have towards others.

PRAYER

Lord Jesus, in you I know the Father's love. Help me to be rooted in the love of God and love of others.
Amen.

Day 4

GOD'S BLESSING MAKES A DIFFERENCE

¹² Isaac sowed seed in that land, and in the same year reaped a hundredfold. The LORD blessed him.
Genesis 26:12

Reflection

Isaac was given land at Gerar, in the territory of the Philistines; a land unfavourable for farming. However, the Lord blessed him, and the land yielded a bountiful harvest to the point that the Philistines became jealous. Dear Child of God, when God's blessing and favour are upon us, even where people fail, we will succeed. Keep in mind that human effort without divine blessing is vain and relying on God without being industrious and prepared is also a sort of foolishness.

PRAYER

Lord Jesus, I surrender all my endeavours to you. May I never labour in vain.
Amen.

YOUR IDENTITY IN CHRIST

⁹ But you are a chosen race, a royal priesthood, a holy nation, God's own people, in order that you may proclaim the mighty acts of Him who called you out of darkness into His marvellous light.

1 Peter 2:9

Reflection

Dear Child of God, we are very significant and important in God's creation. We are part of a race specially chosen. We are one of God's own people, a citizen of a Holy Nation, conferred with the dignity of the baptismal priesthood. The Lord has called us into His wonderful light, and He has prepared for us an eternity of bliss. Let us not be silent; let us declare the greatness of God and proclaim the mighty deeds of Him who has called us from darkness into the light of His love. Let us announce this to others and let us seek to bring others into this kingdom of grace and depopulate the kingdom of darkness.

PRAYER

Lord Jesus, thank you for redeeming me and for bringing me into your wonderful light. May I declare your praise in season and out of season before all people.
Amen.

Day 6

GOD IS MY SALVATION

²Surely God is my salvation; I will trust, and will not be afraid, for the LORD GOD is my strength and my might; He has become my salvation.
Isaiah 12:2

Reflection

Dear Child of God, do not allow anything to plant fear in you. Do not allow anyone or anything to terrify you. The Lord says He is your salvation, He is your strength and your might. All He wants is for you to trust and He will fight your battle and ensure that you are saved.

PRAYER

Lord Jesus, I trust in you; with you as my strength, I know I am safe whatever may betide me. I rest secure in the hollow of your hand. Amen.

YOU SHALL LOVE THE LORD

*³⁰ You shall love the Lord your God with all
your heart, and with all your soul, and with all
your mind, and with all your strength.'*
Mark 12:30

Reflection

Dear Child of God, we do not love God enough if we
do not love Him completely and supremely. We are to
love God with all our faculties. He must be at the
centre of our thoughts, meditation, study and service.
All we do must be done for Him and for His glory. He
must be exalted above everyone else in our lives. When
we love God completely, we are able to love ourselves
accordingly and love others appropriately. No one
enters heaven unless they have proven that they love
God above everyone and everything.

PRAYER

Lord Jesus, you love me to the end. Give me a
heart that seeks and loves you above all else
forever.
Amen.

Day 8

WHEN GOD BLESSES YOU

²⁰See, I received a command to bless; He has blessed, and I cannot revoke it.
Numbers 23:20

Reflection

Balaam was hired by Balak the Moabite king, so that he might curse the Israelites. Balaam instead blessed the people. He said for those God has blessed no one can curse.

Dear Child of God, when God blesses us, no matter how hard anyone tries they can neither curse us nor revoke our blessing. We should not fret about any evil being planned against us or any curse anyone is trying to lay on us. What God has said about us is what matters.

PRAYER

Lord Jesus, thank you for blessing me. Help me to live in the confidence that no one can revoke or destroy what you are doing in my life.
Amen.

ABSTAIN FROM DESIRES OF THE FLESH

[11] Beloved, I urge you as aliens and exiles to abstain from the desires of the flesh that wage war against the soul.
1 Peter 2:11

Reflection

Dear Child of God, the desires of the flesh are always at war with our soul. This is why Jesus exhorted us to practise self-denial for the good of our soul. Let us be careful not to allow the flesh to dominate us. Let us take captive of our feelings and desires and subject them to the law of Christ. It is impossible to please God and attain holiness if we live under the dictatorship of the flesh.

PRAYER

Lord Jesus, help me to mortify my senses and to live according to the new life of grace and not according to sinful instincts.
Amen.

Day 10

A TESTIMONY IS ON THE WAY

10 And the LORD restored the fortunes of Job when he had prayed for his friends; and the LORD gave Job twice as much as he had before.
Job 42:10

Reflection

Dear Child of God, we serve a God of restoration. Job lost all he had and according to human reckoning, his situation was hopeless. However, his end was glorious, and his testimony was great. The Lord restored everything He had lost and gave him honour among his friends, many of whom judged and despised him in his sickness and misery.

When we remain faithful to the Lord throughout our period of crises, we shall have a testimony. We shall sing a new song, and those who have sympathised with us in our misery will marvel at what God will do for us.

PRAYER

Lord Jesus, help me to trust the Father through my crises. May my faith not fail until I receive the full reward of faith and faithfulness.
Amen.

GIVE TO GOD, WHAT IS GOD'S

[25] *He said to them, "Then give to the emperor the things that are the emperor's, and to God the things that are God's."*
Luke 20:25

Reflection

Dear Child of God, faith in God shouldn't be an excuse from fulfilling your civic responsibility and your responsibility to your family. Some people have turned spirituality into an excuse for being rebellious against legitimate authorities and family obligations. Let us keep in mind that we must be respectful of authorities and responsible in our families, except when such commitment demands of us what violates our Christian conscience. It is about knowing boundaries. Our ultimate allegiance is to the Lord because we belong to Him in an absolute sense.

PRAYER

Lord Jesus, help me to respect authorities and to accord you the highest respect when interest clashes.
Amen.

Day 12

BE PATIENT WITH THE WEAK

*⁴ And we urge you, beloved, to admonish the
idlers, encourage the fainthearted, help the
weak, be patient with all of them.*
1 Thessalonians 5:14

Reflection

Dear Child of God, it is very easy to get angry with
people, to rebuke, criticise and judge them. But then,
what does the Lord require of us? He wants us to
encourage the faint-hearted instead of judging them, to
admonish the idlers instead of condemning them, to
help the weak instead of being angry at them and
overall, to be more patient with people.

PRAYER

Lord Jesus, help me to be more patient and
tolerant towards people; turn my short temper
to long suffering.
Amen.

Day 13

GOD IS RICH IN MERCY

*⁴ But God, who is rich in mercy, out of the great love
with which He loved us ⁵ even when we were dead
through our trespasses, made us alive together with
Christ - by grace you have been saved.*

Ephesians 2:4-5

Reflection

Dear Child of God, the message of today should fill us
with so much joy and brighten up our faces.

God loves us so much and He has been generous with
His mercy. God relates to us not according to merit but
according to mercy and grace. Out of His mercy, He
doesn't treat us according to what we deserve. Out of
His grace, He treats us better than we deserve.
Whatever is good in us, what we could have called
merit, is actually His grace at work in us.

Let us therefore not presume that we are made secure
in life by our own intelligence, wealth, strength,
possession or connection, our wise business plans or
future arrangements. Our hope is in His mercy and
without it we are lost. To recognise this is wisdom.
Failure to understand this is spiritual foolishness.

PRAYER

Lord Jesus, my hope is in your mercy. Just as
the eyes of a servant are upon their master, so
my eyes are upon you Lord, untill you show me
mercy.
Amen.

Day 14

BE A BLESSING

*⁹"Blessed be the LORD your God, who has
delighted in you and set you on the throne of
Israel! Because the LORD loved Israel forever,
He has made you king to execute justice and
righteousness."*
1 Kings 10:9

Reflection

The queen of Sheba marvelled at the wisdom of
Solomon and blessed the Lord His God. She
acknowledged that Solomon was a blessing of God to
the people and she reminded him why God had made
him king - to execute justice and righteousness. Dear
Child of God, make every effort to be a blessing to the
people amongst whom the Lord your God has placed
you. Remember why you are where you are. It is not
for you to promote your own interest but the interest
of God and to add value to the lives of others.

PRAYER

Lord Jesus, make me a blessing in my family, in
the Church and in my place of work, among my
friends and my colleagues.
Amen.

Day 15

DO EVERYTHING IN THE NAME OF THE LORD

*¹⁷ And whatever you do, in word or deed, do
everything in the name of the Lord Jesus, giving
thanks to God the Father through Him.*
Colossians 3:17

Reflection

Dear Child of God, the Lord wants you to do whatever
you are meant to do, but not for the sake of promoting
your own name or to please anyone. Whatever you are
expected to do, whatever your responsibilities are,
work at it with the aim that you are doing them for God
and to give Him glory. Turn your duty to worship,
your work to service and your task to thanksgiving.

PRAYER

Lord Jesus, thank you for all I am able to do.
May I do this with the aim of honouring you and
giving thanks for your great glory.
Amen.

Day 16

DEATH IS ONCE

27 And just as it is appointed for mortals to die
once, and after that the judgment.
Hebrews 9:27

Reflection

Dear Child of God, we are not meant to live forever in
this world. It is appointed for us to depart at a time we
do not know. Every funeral we attend, every news of
death that we hear should always serve as a reminder
to us that we are mortal, that we shall sleep and wake
at the other side one day, and that we shall part from
our loved ones one day. When this happens, we shall
have to render account to God. If our account is not
balanced, it is impossible to come back and set things
in order. We shall have to deal with the consequences.
Let us keep this in mind and prepare for the inevitable.

PRAYER

Lord Jesus, by dying you destroyed our death,
and by rising you restored our life. Remove from
my heart the fear of death but give me the grace
to put my life in order and to prepare to meet
you whenever you call me.
Amen.

Day 17

LET YOUR SPEECH BE GRACIOUS

⁶Let your speech always be gracious, seasoned with salt, so that you may know how you ought to answer everyone.
Colossians 4:6

Reflection

Our choice of words is a good measure of our character and our spiritual maturity. Dear Child of God, the Lord wants us to scrutinise whatever comes out of our mouths. We must speak words that are true and that will bring joy, encouragement and life to those who hear us. We must answer everyone with calmness, wisdom and grace, and not allow ourselves to be provoked to speak harshly or out of fury to anyone.

PRAYER

Lord Jesus, sanctify my tongue that it may speak only of your love and your word of grace. Amen.

Day 18

OUR PRIDE IS IN GOD'S NAME

[7] Some take pride in chariots, and some in horses, but our pride is in the name of the Lord our God.
Psalm 20:7

Reflection

Many people boast of their power, friends, jobs, material possessions, their success, their looks and their intelligence. All these are temporal and unreliable. In fact, these are gifted to us by God, the giver of all that is good. Dear Child of God, we should let our boast be in the Lord our God. We should boast of His name, and that we belong to Him. We should boast of His work of redemption. We should place our hope of salvation in Him. It is only in Him that our life has meaning, and His mercy is our hope.

PRAYER

Lord Jesus, may I not boast in what is insignificant in life but rather rejoice in the joy that I belong to you and in the hope of salvation that I have in you.
Amen.

Day 19

OBEDIENCE IS BETTER THAN SACRIFICE

²² And Samuel said, "Has the Lord as great delight in burnt offerings and sacrifices, as in obedience to the voice of the Lord? Surely, to obey is better than sacrifice, and to heed than the fat of rams."
1 Samuel 15:22

Reflection

Dear Child of God, to obey the Lord is the greatest sacrifice we can render Him. It is obedience to the Lord that makes all our activities, service, worship and prayers meaningful and acceptable. An obedient heart is a heart that gives God due worship and praise. When we claim to love the Lord and serve Him, but we live our lives going against His will, we make our service and worship unacceptable.

PRAYER

Lord Jesus, the sacrifice you demand of me is to first bow in obedience and to do your will. Help me to set aside my stubbornness and be willing to do that which is pleasing to you, even if my weak nature protests against it.
Amen.

Day 20

I PRESS ON

*12 Not that I have already obtained this or have
already reached the goal; but I press on to make
it my own, because Christ Jesus has made me
His own.*
Philippians 3:12

Reflection

Dear Child of God, as long as we are in this world, we
cannot claim that we have reached our goal and that
heaven is sure for us. When we are in the flesh, the
battle continues. We are still tempted to sin, to disobey
God, to choose wrongly, to follow other paths.
However, let us not be tired of making progress and
focusing on Jesus. Let us press forward without losing
heart, focusing on the joy that lies ahead of us.

PRAYER

Lord Jesus, save me from presuming that I
cannot fall. Help me to keep making an effort
without being wearied. Help me to keep my
focus on you and the reward of eternal life with
you.
Amen.

Day 21

THE GOD WHO OBSERVES

⁷ Then the Lord said, "I have observed the misery of my people who are in Egypt; I have heard their cry on account of their taskmasters. Indeed, I know their sufferings."
Exodus 3:7

Reflection

Dear Child of God, our God is a God who sees, observes and knows everything. He is not aloof and uninterested in what we go through. He told Moses that He had seen the misery of His people in Egypt. He had heard their cry and He knew their suffering. Keep in mind today, God sees our struggles and our hidden tears. He hears our cries and prayers. He knows our suffering and He will help us.

PRAYER

Lord Jesus, I am content that you know all about my struggles and pains and to you I look for help. Make haste to help me; save me lest I perish.

Amen.

Day 22

TAKE NO OFFENCE IN THE LORD

*"And blessed is anyone who takes
no offense at me."*
Matthew 11:6

Reflection

When John the Baptist was in prison, he expected Jesus to come quickly and liberate him but instead of that, he heard that Jesus was busy ministering to others. That upset his faith and so he sent his disciples to Jesus to ask if he was truly the Messiah or were they to expect another. Jesus simply replied by sending them back to tell John what they had seen Him doing and He ended by leaving this message for John, *Blessed is anyone who takes no offence at me.* This means, blessed is anyone who doesn't lose faith in Jesus.

Dear Child of God, you may be in a situation that is causing you to doubt many things but let the words of Jesus to John be amplified in your heart - "blessed is anyone who does not lose faith in Jesus."

PRAYER

Lord Jesus, no matter what I go through, may I be steadfast in my faith and never give in to doubt.
Amen.

DO NOT RETURN TO SIN

*20 For if, after they have escaped the defilements
of the world through the knowledge of our Lord
and Saviour Jesus Christ, they are again
entangled in them and overpowered, the last
state has become worse for them than the first.*
2 Peter 2:20

Reflection

Whenever we repent of our sins and make confession, we enter into a realm of freedom and grace. We receive the peace of being freed from guilt and condemnation. This is a state that the devil doesn't want any Child of God to be in. He does everything possible to make us go back to committing those sins again and again. Whenever we make a resolution to follow the Lord, the enemy comes after us with strong temptations and trials to make us go back to our old life of sin.

Dear Child of God, keep in mind the Word of God today. If after being sanctified and justified, we go back and sin again, we enter into a deeper realm of bondage because the enemy binds us stronger than before.

PRAYER

Lord Jesus, I have decided to follow you on the road to life. May I not turn back but keep marching forward with you.

Amen.

Day 24

HE GAVE GIFTS TO PEOPLE

[8] Therefore it is said, "When He ascended on high He made captivity itself a captive; He gave gifts to His people."
Ephesians 4:8

Reflection

After the ascension of Jesus, He sent the greatest gift to His disciples - the Holy Spirit. With the Holy Spirit they received a variety of gifts to be used in His service. Each one of us has also received gifts from God through the power of the Holy Spirit. We have been blessed with gifts and graces to be used for the service of others and for the building of the body of Christ. Dear Child of God, do you use your gifts productively for God's glory? Do you allow the Holy Spirit to help you to develop your gifts? Are you helping others through the gifts God has bestowed upon you?

PRAYER

Lord Jesus, you bestow your gift of grace upon me. Help me to use what I have received according to your will and pleasure.
Amen.

Day 25
BE CAREFUL WHAT YOU SOW

¹⁶ You shall not go around as a slanderer among your people, and you shall not profit by the blood of your neighbour: I am the Lord.
Leviticus 19:16

Reflection

Dear Child of God, whatever you do today is like sowing seed. It will germinate and you shall reap it eventually. Anyone who slanders others will suffer the same fate. Anyone who seeks profit through the downfall of others will also reap what he/she is sowing. Be careful what you sow today. Do not sow the seed of slander or evil, so that you don't regret when you reap.

PRAYER

Lord Jesus, help me to carefully avoid slandering anyone. As I wish that my integrity be preserved, may I never be eager to tarnish that of another.
Amen.

Day 26

JOY IN TRIALS

*² My brothers and sisters, whenever you face trials of
any kind, consider it nothing but joy, ³ because you
know that the testing of your faith produces endurance;
⁴ and let endurance have its full effect, so that you may
be mature and complete, lacking in nothing.*
James 1:2-4

Reflection

Dear Child of God, trials are inevitable in life. We all
face trials of our values, beliefs and purpose in life. As
much as we can't avoid trials, we can choose our
response to it. We may decide to be beaten, broken and
discouraged, or we can decide to adopt the attitude of
a victor. We can refuse to be broken and see our
challenges in an optimistic sense. This is what St.
James proposes. We can choose to face our trials with
joy and the strength that God provides, keeping in
mind that when our approach is right, our trials will
leave us better and not bitter, stronger and not
defeated.

PRAYER

Lord Jesus, help me to become stronger and
better and not beaten and bitter through my
trials.
Amen.

HOLD FAST TO THE LORD

20 Loving the Lord your God, obeying Him, and holding fast to Him; for that means life to you and length of days, so that you may live in the land that the Lord swore to give to your ancestors, to Abraham, to Isaac, and to Jacob.
Deuteronomy 30:20

Reflection

Dear Child of God, you are reminded of three things today - love the Lord, obey Him and hold fast to Him. Let us pause for a while and digest the injunction to hold fast to the Lord. It means let nothing come between you and your God. Carry Him with you wherever you go, and do not let your eyes turn away from Him. This is the way to live a meaningful and blessed life in this world and in the world to come.

PRAYER

Lord Jesus, I cling to you, I hold fast to you. Separate me from whatever threatens to separate me from you.
Amen.

Day 28

TURN TO HIM IN REPENTANCE

[14] If my people who are called by my name humble themselves, pray, seek my face, and turn from their wicked ways, then I will hear from heaven, and will forgive their sin and heal their land.
2 Chronicles 7:14

Reflection

Dear Child of God, God has given us His word. He is willing to forgive whatever sins we have committed and to remove whatever guilt is in our hearts. He wants to heal the effect of our sins. What does He require from us? We must be humble enough to admit that we have sinned. We must be humble enough not to justify our sins or excuse ourselves but to accept responsibility. We must be willing to make amends by turning away from sin and turning to Him in repentance.

PRAYER

Lord Jesus, give me a humble and a contrite heart. Help me to despise what the Father despises. Make me aware of the damage that sin can cause to me, and may I not stay a minute longer in it.
Amen.

Day 29

LOVE COVERS OFFENCES

12 Hatred stirs up strife,
but love covers all offenses.
Proverbs 10:12

Reflection

When we hate someone, we find fault in them. We suspect all that they do, we become irrational and act in a way unbefitting of children of God.

Dear Child of God, hatred is a deadly virus in the body of those created in God's image. It corrupts our thoughts and disorientates our actions. Let us instead allow love to grow within us. Love in us is the beauty of our soul.

PRAYER

Lord Jesus, cleanse me of all hatred and adorn my soul with the fragrance of love.
Amen.

Day 30

WE DO NOT LIVE FOR OURSELVES

⁷ We do not live to ourselves, and we do not die to ourselves.
Romans 14:7

Reflection

Dear Child of God, do not say "It is my life, I can do what I like with it." Did you will yourself into existence? The life in you is a gift from God and you are fundamentally related to others. Your choices and actions have an effect not just on you but on others. Keep this in mind before making any significant decisions. Ask yourself, "Will God, the owner of my life, be pleased with this decision or action? What effect will this have on those to whom I am related and those who care about me?"

PRAYER

Lord Jesus, help me to keep in mind that my life is not mine alone but principally a gift from you and you want me to be a gift from you to others too.
Amen.

MAY

Day 1

BE STRONG IN THE LORD

¹⁰ Finally, be strong in the Lord and in the strength of His power.
Ephesians 6:10

Reflection

Dear Child of God, the Lord has given you the grace to deal with every circumstance, the power to overcome every battle, and the strength to reach your goal. Declare positively about yourself, do not live a life of self-pity, do not live like a victim, do not live your life as someone defeated and powerless. No matter what your trials may be, remain strong in the Lord and in the strength of His might.

PRAYER

Lord Jesus, thank you for giving me strength, and thank you for your grace in my life. May I live this day in the strength you have supplied. Amen.

BE STEADFAST AND EXCEL IN GOD'S WORK

[58] Therefore, my beloved, be steadfast, immovable, always excelling in the work of the Lord, because you know that in the Lord your labour is not in vain.
1 Corinthians 15:58

Reflection

Dear Child of God, we should dig our heels in our service to the Lord and let no one discourage us. We should work for the Lord joyfully and excel humbly in whatever we do for the spread of God's kingdom and the growth of the Church. We must keep in mind that our labour for the Lord can never be in vain. Everything we do for the Lord is noted for eternal recompense.

PRAYER

Lord Jesus, thank you for counting me worthy to serve you. Keep me focused, joyful and unmoved in working for you. Show me new ways that you need me, and I will not hesitate to surrender myself.
Amen.

Day 3

GOD WILL FIGHT FOR YOU

⁴ for it is the Lord your God who goes with you, to fight for you against your enemies, to give you victory.
Deuteronomy 20:4

Reflection

Dear Child of God, the Lord says He will always go with us, He will fight for us, He will give us victory. Are you being threatened by anyone? Do you feel you are in a strange battle? Are you being unjustly treated, falsely accused, victimised, suffering from acts of injustice? Is your right withheld or denied? Do not let your soul be downcast, you have a defender, call on Him. He says, "He will fight for you and give you victory."

PRAYER

Lord Jesus, I know that you are always with me to give me victory. May I keep this in mind always and never be tempted to feel helpless and forlorn.
Amen.

Day 4

GOD MOVED PEOPLE FOR HIS PURPOSE

¹ In the first year of King Cyrus of Persia, in order that the Word of the Lord by the mouth of Jeremiah might be accomplished, the Lord stirred up the spirit of King Cyrus of Persia so that he sent a herald throughout all his kingdom....
Ezra 1:1

Reflection

Dear Child of God, if the Lord has promised us anything, if we are waiting on Him for something, we should not bother ourselves thinking on how He will do it, because His ways are beyond our human reasoning. To fulfil His promise through the prophet Jeremiah, He stirred the heart of Cyrus, the King of Persia to issue a decree that a temple of Jerusalem be rebuilt. Who could ever have thought this would come from the pagan king of Persia? When the time is right, God acts in mysterious ways. He moved the heart of Cyrus to favour His people, may He move the spirit of those who will favour us.

PRAYER

Lord Jesus, help me trust in the omnipotent power of God. When I trust, my heart can rest assured because He is a God who never fails. Amen.

130

Day 5

WATCH THAT YOU DO NOT FALL

¹² So if you think you are standing, watch out that you do not fall.
1 Corinthians 10:12

Reflection

Dear Child of God, let us be careful how we live our lives and not presume too much on our strength. Many are those who thought they were strong but fell too soon to sin. Be careful to resist the thought of sin at the first suggestion and do not plunge yourself in an occasion of sin. Guard your soul jealously and pray to God fervently. If we become careless with our souls, the adversary will spare no opportunity to steal, to kill and destroy.

PRAYER

Lord Jesus, help me to be careful of how I order my life even as I rely on you for guidance. May I not plunge myself where my soul will be in great danger.
Amen.

THE EGYPTIANS YOU SEE TODAY

13 But Moses said to the people, "Do not be afraid, stand firm, and see the deliverance that the Lord will accomplish for you today; for the Egyptians whom you see today you shall never see again. 14 The Lord will fight for you, and you have only to keep still."
Exodus 14:13-14

Reflection

Dear Child of God, just as the Lord told the Israelites not to be afraid, He is telling us today not to be afraid. He is with us, we are safe in the hollow of His hands. The cause of our fear today will become a forgotten story soon. He will sort us out, our mountain shall melt before us, and what we see as a problem today shall become our testimony tomorrow. When the Lord is fighting our battle, we only have to keep still and stand firm in Him.

PRAYER

Lord Jesus, I thank you in faith because I know that my cause of fear today shall exist no more when I stand firm in you and allow you to sort me out.
Amen.

Day 7

WE ARE NOT TO PLEASE OURSELVES

¹ We who are strong ought to put up with the failings of the weak, and not to please ourselves.

Romans 15:1

Reflection

Dear Child of God, everyone is not at the same stage in their spiritual life. Some of us are strong and some of us are weak. Our strength and weakness aren't the same, but our common denominator is that we are all imperfect, we are fallible, and we all rely on God's grace. As such, if you feel strong, please do not judge or condemn those who are weak or not as strong. If you feel weak, do not be discouraged when you see the strong doing amazing things. What is most important to the Lord is our effort at pleasing Him and our love for one another.

PRAYER

Lord Jesus, help me to be more patient, tolerant, kind and understanding to others, especially those who are weaker and struggling differently from me.
Amen.

MY GRACE IS SUFFICIENT FOR YOU

⁹ But He said to me, "My grace is sufficient for you, for power is made perfect in weakness." So, I will boast all the more gladly of my weaknesses, so that the power of Christ may dwell in me. ¹⁰ Therefore I am content with weaknesses, insults, hardships, persecutions, and calamities for the sake of Christ; for whenever I am weak, then I am strong.

2 Corinthians 12:9-10

Reflection

Dear Child of God, do you feel weak and unable to carry out a task before you? Do you feel powerless in the face of what you are confronted with? Do you feel overwhelmed by everything happening in your life and around you? Listen to what the Lord is saying to you, "My grace is sufficient for you." The Lord's grace is sufficient for whatever you have to do or face or go through. Call on God for His grace and you will receive strength to carry on stronger and better. No challenge is ever greater than the strength of His grace.

PRAYER

Lord Jesus, thank you for your grace which I have received as an undeserved gift. By the power of your grace, may I soar above my obstacles.
Amen.

Day 9

HE WHO HAS PROMISED IS FAITHFUL

²³ Let us hold fast to the confession of our hope without wavering, for he who has promised is faithful.
Hebrews 10:23

Reflection

Our hope in God gives us the strength to forge ahead in life. Our hope in His promises renews our strength. Therefore, let us continue relying on Him with the assurance that people may promise and fail but God is absolutely faithful. Dear Child of God, we cannot be disappointed by God. Even though things are unstable and unclear at the moment, let us march forward with hope, live each day in hope and never give in to despair.

PRAYER

Lord Jesus, I hope in you for grace and favour because of your promise, your love and your power.
Amen.

Day 10

REJOICE IN HOPE

[12] Rejoice in hope, be patient in suffering,
persevere in prayer.
Romans 12:12

Reflection

Dear Child of God, these three counsels are important as we go through the hurdles of life.

- Keep rejoicing in the hope you have in God. We are not hopeless or helpless. All things are working together for our good - this is our hope.
- Be patient in suffering because it will not last forever. It is a phase and it will end in our favour.
- Persevere in prayer because it is only through the strength that comes from prayers that we can emerge victorious and strong.

PRAYER

Lord Jesus, help me to rejoice in hope, to be patient in moments of adversity and to persevere in fervent prayers.
Amen.

Day 11

DO NOT WORRY ABOUT TOMORROW

> [34] "So do not worry about tomorrow, for
> tomorrow will bring worries of its own.
> Today's trouble is enough for today.
> **Matthew 6:34**

Reflection

Dear Child of God, the Lord has not called us into a life of fear, worry and anxiety. He has called us to a life of trust and faithfulness, a life of peace and joy in the Spirit. When we surrender to the Lord, He purifies our past, blesses our present and takes care of our tomorrow. Let us not spend today living in yesterday and worrying about tomorrow, whilst we allow the wonder of today to pass us by. Let your song be "because He lives, I can face tomorrow."

PRAYER

Lord Jesus, thank you for my past, and thank you for today. Thank you that I can hope in you for a brighter tomorrow.
Amen.

DO NOT GROW WEARY OF DOING WHAT IS RIGHT

⁹ So let us not grow weary in doing what is right, for we will reap at harvest time, if we do not give up.
Galatians 6:9

Reflection

Dear Child of God, sometimes we are tempted to give up something good. Sometimes we feel we are not appreciated, or our good deed is unnoticed, unneeded or insignificant. Keep the Word of God in mind today, and do not grow weary in doing what is right. Let us continue doing what we know to be right, because we shall reap a good harvest only if we do not give up.

PRAYER

Lord Jesus, give me the grace to continue the good you have called me to do. May I never give up until I receive the reward of those who persevere to the end.
Amen.

Day 13

SOMETHING MORE THAN SILVER OR GOLD

⁶ But Peter said, "I have no silver or gold, but what I have I give you; in the name of Jesus Christ of Nazareth, stand up and walk."
Acts 3:6

Reflection

Many people in our world think money is everything. Money has definitely been overrated. Many things are measured in terms of their monetary worth. Many people think without money they can't be happy. Money is at the centre of their thoughts and consideration. Today, we see how Peter and John, even though they didn't have money, gave something money can't buy. Dear Child of God, money is not everything. Do not put on a furrowed brow because you lack money. Do not think you have nothing to give to others because you have no money in your pocket. You have words of encouragement to lift someone up, a smile to cheer someone's heart and lighten someone's face, good advice to save someone from going the wrong way, and you have the Good News to restore someone back to true life.

PRAYER

Lord Jesus, open my eyes to see the hidden riches you have bestowed on me and that you have called me to share with others.
Amen.

Day 14

NO TEMPTATION BEYOND YOUR STRENGTH

[13] No testing has overtaken you that is not common to everyone. God is faithful, and He will not let you be tested beyond your strength, but with the testing He will also provide the way out so that you may be able to endure it.
1 Corinthians 10:13

Reflection

Dear Child of God, let these words comfort and reassure you. God will never allow us to be tempted beyond our strength and for any temptation we face, He will also provide a way out for us. Whatever temptation you are facing now, do not surrender to it, do not be overwhelmed by it, do not feel hopeless and helpless. Keep on fighting, keep on resisting, be firm in your resolution. God says He won't allow you to be consumed. He will provide a way out for you.

PRAYER

Lord Jesus, I trust in you that I will not face a temptation that you and I cannot handle. Give me the strength to overcome every temptation that might come my way this day and always. Amen.

Day 15

PEACE I GIVE YOU

²⁷ Peace I leave with you; my peace I give to you. I do not give to you as the world gives. Do not let your hearts be troubled, and do not let them be afraid.

John 14:27

Reflection

Dear Child of God, Jesus promises us peace; a peace not like the world gives. He says we should guard our hearts against being troubled and afraid. Peace is both a gift and a responsibility. Christ has won peace for us, but we must also work hard to avoid whatever may endanger it. Sin threatens our peace of mind. When we are unfair or unkind to others, our peace is disturbed. When we listen to the wrong voices, our peace is troubled. When we open our hearts to hatred, resentment and unforgiveness, we lose our peace. Let us therefore do all we can to preserve the heavenly peace that Jesus brings to us.

PRAYER

Lord Jesus, thank you for the gift of peace. May I preserve this gift through your help and may nothing take away your peace in my heart. Amen.

141

LIVE PEACEABLY WITH ALL

*¹⁸ If it is possible, so far as it depends on
you, live peaceably with all.*
Romans 12:18

Reflection

It is difficult to be at peace with some people, no matter
how hard we try. Sometimes the Spirit of God in us
provokes the spirit dwelling in some people. This is
why the Word of God says if it's possible, so far as it
depends on you, live peaceably with everyone. Let us
not be lovers of malice and grudges. Let us be lovers of
peace and be quick to reconcile and prevent any seed
of resentment from growing within us. Our heart must
be at peace even with those who do not love us,
holding nothing against them. God wants us to seek to
be at peace with Him and with others.

PRAYER

Lord Jesus Christ, help me to cherish peace and
to do my best to live peaceably with others.
Amen.

Day 17

FAITH IS THE CONVICTION OF WHAT IS UNSEEN

*¹Now faith is the assurance of things hoped
for, the conviction of things not seen.*
Hebrews 11:1

Reflection

Faith is very important in our relationship with God.
It is by faith that we walk with God. It is by faith that
we believe what He has said and promised. It is by faith
that we obey God knowing that what He asks of us is
for our good. Faith is trusting in who God says He is
and in what He says He will do. It is the assurance that
we shall receive what He has promised and the
certainty of what we have not seen. Faith is a gift of
God and it is a currency that can obtain for us anything
from the store of good things in heaven. Let us always
pray for increase in our faith. In most cases, we receive
favour from the Lord according to the extent of our
faith.

PRAYER

Lord Jesus, increase my faith in you. Let me
never doubt what you have said and promised.
Amen.

Day 18

VENGEANCE IS MINE

19 Beloved, never avenge yourselves, but leave room for the wrath of God; for it is written, "Vengeance is mine, I will repay, says the Lord."

Romans 12:19

Reflection

Dear Child of God, has anyone hurt or wrong you? Are you feeling bad about it? Do you feel like retaliating the ill done? The thought of retaliation is not from God. It is the evil one trying to manipulate our minds. The Lord doesn't want us to repay evil with evil. Instead, He says vengeance is mine. If vengeance is for the Lord and we decide to take vengeance on someone, it means we are competing with God and equating ourselves with Him. If you feel hurt by anyone, do not try to harm them back. Allow God to decide. Do not even wish them evil, this is not the Spirit of Christ. However, it is wisdom to prevent ourselves from further harm by such people.

PRAYER

Lord Jesus, you are never tired of showing me mercy. May I show the same mercy to others just as you have shown to me. Take away from me every desire for revenge.
Amen.

Day 19

I SEE HEAVEN OPENED

⁵⁵ But filled with the Holy Spirit, he gazed into heaven and saw the glory of God and Jesus standing at the right hand of God. ⁵⁶ "Look," he said, "I see the heavens opened and the Son of Man standing at the right hand of God!"
Acts 7:55-56

Reflection

Stephen gazed into heaven and he saw Jesus standing at the right hand of God. Stephen lived his life witnessing to Jesus. At death's hour, he was blessed to have a glimpse of the glory of heaven. He saw Jesus standing to welcome him, to receive his soul, and with this sight, dying lost its terror. When we live for Christ and we die testifying to the Lord, He will testify to us before His Father. He will reveal Himself to us at the hour of our death. He will stand to welcome us into the joy of His kingdom. This is when death is a real gain.

PRAYER

Lord Jesus, may I live for you and see you before I see death.
Amen.

Day 20

REJOICE ALWAYS

16 Rejoice always.
1 Thessalonians 5:16

Reflection

Dear Child of God, the enemy wants us to always be miserable, to always be bitter, to hate ourselves, to be unhappy within ourselves, to spend our days sulking and in frustration and when we come to our wits' end, to end our life in sorrow. The Lord wants us to rejoice and be happy. The choice is ours. We should choose to live for God, trusting in His love for us and living each day rejoicing until we cross to the other side where there will be no end to our rejoicing.

PRAYER

Lord Jesus, I accept your joy, and I choose to rejoice. I declare that I shall not spend my time on earth in lamentation but in praising your goodness unceasingly.
Amen.

Day 21

REBELLION RUINS SPIRITUALITY

²Therefore whoever resists authority, resists what God has appointed, and those who resist will incur judgment.
Romans 13:2

Reflection

Dear Child of God, do not allow rebellion to ruin your spirituality. Many are those who are always rebellious against authorities - both religious and secular authorities. They are always accusing Church leaders and they are anti-government. They see everything wrong with the hierarchy of the Church and holders of public office. The Spirit of God is the Spirit of truth and justice, not opposition and antagonism. The spirituality that doesn't accept authority or sees everything wrong in every authority, is questionable.

PRAYER

Lord Jesus, teach me submission to authorities that you have constituted. May I obey them in all that is right.
Amen.

Day 22

PUT AWAY YOUR OLD SELF

*²² You were taught to put away your former
way of life, your old self, corrupt and
deluded by its lusts.*
Ephesians 4:22

Reflection

Dear Child of God, redeemed by the sacrifice of Jesus
and called to the family of God's holy people, we are
called to put away our old self, our old habits, our old
appetite and desires. We are to put on the righteousness
of Christ, His character, His Spirit. We are to become
new. Let us not come into the household of God's
people with the old and corrupt self. New wine
deserves new wineskin.

PRAYER

Lord Jesus, help me to cast off any old habit of
sin and corruption and be renewed in mind and
body, taking upon myself the righteousness
which is yours.
Amen.

Day 23

NO FALSE WITNESS

¹⁶ You shall not bear false witness against your neighbour.
Exodus 20:16

Reflection

Dear Child of God, you are called to love and to seek the good of others. Avoid whatever offends others and avoid any act of injustice and lack of charity to others. Do not be persuaded or threatened to witness against anyone on what you are unsure of or what you know is not true. Be protective of the integrity of others and do not let anyone suffer unjustly because of you.

PRAYER

Lord Jesus, help me to avoid any act of injustice against anyone. May I never bear false witness against others or slander them for any reason. Amen.

Day 24

GOD WILL FULFIL HIS PROMISE IN HIS TIME

[10] For thus says the Lord: Only when Babylon's seventy years are completed will I visit you, and I will fulfil to you my promise and bring you back to this place.
Jeremiah 29:10

Reflection

The Lord has a plan for His people. It is a wonderful plan. They want it fulfilled sooner than immediately but God will never bow to their pressure or work with their time. He planned to liberate His people but not until after seventy years. Dear Child of God, God knows what He has in mind for you and He knows the perfect time. Don't be impatient, hasty or desperate. When we become desperate for anything, we make ourselves very vulnerable and susceptible to temptations.

PRAYER

Lord Jesus, I know the Father has a wonderful plan for me. Teach me patience and trust so that I may joyfully receive what has been bountifully prepared for me.
Amen.

Day 25

COVENANT KEEPING GOD

*⁵ I said, "O Lord God of heaven, the great
and awesome God who keeps covenant and
steadfast love with those who love Him and
keep His commandments;*
Nehemiah 1:5

Reflection

Dear Child of God, our God is a covenant keeping
God. He is a promise keeper, and He is an awesome
God. He is loving and faithful in all His ways. Those
who love Him and keep His commandments dispose
themselves to experience more of His goodness. To
such an awesome God, to such a promise keeper, our
response should just be to worship and praise Him and
the highest form of worship is obedience. As we
worship God as a covenant keeping God, let us also
remember that we ought to imitate Him by being
faithful to our covenant and promise to Him.

PRAYER

Lord Jesus, in you, mankind entered a new
covenant with the Father, a covenant sealed by
your blood. Help me to be faithful to this
covenant of grace by living in obedience to you
and loving what you command.
Amen.

Day 26

EVERY WORD OF GOD IS TRUE

⁵ Every Word of God proves true; He is a shield to those who take refuge in Him.
Proverbs 30:5

Reflection

People often say what they do not mean. Many say words that are not true, words that are misleading and confusing. Dear Child of God, the Word of God is not like this. The Word of God is true, it is dependable, it is infallible and powerful. Stand on the promise of God's Word and you will be standing on a solid foundation. Drink from the fountain of God's Holy Word and your soul shall be satisfied.

PRAYER

Lord Jesus, I confess that your Word is true, and it revives the soul. Give me more understanding of your Word that growing in your Word, I may find comfort and hope.
Amen.

Day 27

ABSTAIN FROM EVIL

22 ....abstain from every form of evil.
1 Thessalonians 5:22

Reflection

Dear Child of God, this is a powerful counsel for us. We must abstain from every form or appearance of evil. We must not be found where evil is being planned, executed or celebrated. We must never be among those apprehended or chastised for misconduct. We must not silence our conscience when it warns us of evil or try to be tolerant of wrong doing. Let us abstain, run away and never be party to any form of evil plan, deed or scheme.

PRAYER

Lord Jesus, you are all good and from you comes all that is good. Help me to discern and refuse all that is evil and offensive to your goodness. Amen.

Day 28

NOTHING THAT THE LORD CANNOT DO

*14 Is anything too wonderful for the Lord?
At the set time I will return to you, in due
season, and Sarah shall have a son."*
Genesis 18:14

Reflection

Sarah was told she would have a child in her old age.
She laughed because it seemed impossible, unnatural
and ridiculous. She could not get her head around the
promise. She desperately wanted a child, but she was
so sure it was no longer possible. She was told that
nothing is impossible for God. The promise strained
her credulity to breaking point. The fulfilment left her
completely dumbfounded. Dear Child of God, these
words were spoken to Sarah, and the Lord speaks them
to you today: "There is nothing too wonderful for me
to do. I surprised Sarah, I will surprise you too."

PRAYER

Lord Jesus, I believe that nothing is impossible
for God, He only has to will it. I surrender my
needs to Him, and I believe that He will act in
my favour and He will surprise me with His
mercy.
Amen.

Day 29

BE ROOTED AND BUILT UP IN CHRIST

⁶ As you therefore have received Christ Jesus the Lord, continue to live your lives in Him, ⁷ rooted and built up in Him and established in the faith, just as you were taught, abounding in thanksgiving.
Colossians 2:6-7

Reflection

Dear Child of God, the greatest gift we have in life is the gift of faith in Christ Jesus. This should, in each moment, fill us with joy and thanksgiving. It is our bounden duty therefore, to continue to live our lives in Him, to be rooted and built up in Him, to be established in Him as a plant grafted to another. Let us keep in mind that Christ is the vine and we are the branches. When we stay with Him, we receive nutrients and energy to blossom. When we allow ourselves to drift from Him, we wither and become a waste.

PRAYER

Lord Jesus, may nothing in this world ever separate me from you, for in you is the source of my life and being.
Amen.

THE PRAYER OF FAITH

12 On the day when the Lord gave the Amorites over to the Israelites, Joshua spoke to the Lord; and he said in the sight of Israel, "Sun, stand still at Gibeon, and Moon, in the valley of Aijalon." 13 And the sun stood still, and the moon stopped, until the nation took vengeance on their enemies. Is this not written in the Book of Jashar? The sun stopped in midheaven and did not hurry to set for about a whole day.
Joshua 10:12-13

Reflection

Joshua commanded the moon and the sun to stand still and they obeyed. The Lord honoured His words and performed a miracle of nature at the words of Joshua. Dear Child of God, prayers of faith are very powerful. A good life also adds efficacy to our prayers. When we honour God by our lives, He honours our words. When our lives glorify God, He manifests His greatness through us.

PRAYER

Lord Jesus, you only have to say the word and what you have spoken comes to be. May my life honour you in every way so that my words shall be acceptable in your sight as well.
Amen.

Day 31
THE UNITY OF THE SPIRIT

² Be completely humble and gentle; be patient, bearing with one another in love. ³ Make every effort to keep the unity of the Spirit through the bond of peace.
Ephesians 4:2-3

Reflection

St. Paul encourages us to preserve the unity of the Spirit. Dear Child of God, our coming together and fellowship in the Church, despite our different backgrounds, is the work of the Holy Spirit. The Lord didn't command us to create unity, He has created it by His Spirit. He only commands us to recognise it and keep it. How do we keep this? St. Paul tells us to learn to bear with one another charitably, in complete selflessness, gentleness and patience. Let us cooperate with the Holy Spirit to foster unity in the Church, knowing that we are united with others by the same baptism. We received the same Spirit, we all share the same faith, we look forward to the same hope and serve the same Christ.

PRAYER

Lord Jesus, help me to recognise and appreciate the work of the Holy Spirit in the lives of others in the Church. May I work to preserve the unity of the Spirit.
Amen.

JUNE

Day 1

PRAY WITHOUT CEASING

[17] Pray without ceasing.
1 Thessalonians 5:17

Reflection

Dear Child of God, the Lord wants you to make prayers an important part of your life and your day. Let your minds be perpetually lifted up to the Lord. Let prayer accompany whatever you do. Do everything with the consciousness of God's presence and in the spirit of love. Where love is present, God is present. When we make God present and we are conscious of His presence, everything becomes a prayer. This is how we pray without ceasing.

PRAYER

Lord Jesus, prayer was an integral part of your ministry. Help me to cultivate a spirit of prayer and a constant awareness of God's loving presence around me.
Amen.

Day 2

OUR COMPETENCE IS FROM GOD

*⁵ Not that we are competent of ourselves to
claim anything as coming from us; our
competence is from God.*
2 Corinthians 3:5

Reflection

Dear Child of God, a recognition that all good gifts in us and around us are from God is an evidence of wisdom. This wisdom leads to humility and humility puts us in a place of favour before God who resists the proud but favours the lowly. Do not boast of anything in you and do not treat others with contempt. Keep in mind that all we have received is a gift of grace for the glory of God and the service of others.

PRAYER

Lord Jesus, thank you for all you have bestowed on me through your Spirit. Keep my heart from boasting and my soul from pride.
Amen.

Day 3

HONOUR TO WHOM HONOUR IS DUE

7 Pay to all what is due them—taxes to whom taxes are due, revenue to whom revenue is due, respect to whom respect is due, honour to whom honour is due.
Romans 13:7

Reflection

Dear Child of God, the Lord wants you to be faithful in fulfilling your civic responsibilities. He also wants you to give honour to whom honour is due. Keep in mind that honour and respect are due to our leaders, both religious and civil, our parents, guardians, those whom God has placed over us and those whom God has positioned to teach us. However, honour is due to everyone created by God because we are all bearers of the divine image. See to it that you do not dishonour or disrespect any of God's creatures. Do not be provoked to act towards anyone without charity and respect.

PRAYER

Lord Jesus, may I give honour to everyone I meet and may I give you highest honour in my life.
Amen.

Day 4

A LIFE WORTHY OF YOUR CALL

*¹ I therefore, the prisoner in the Lord, beg you
to lead a life worthy of the calling to which
you have been called.*
Ephesians 4:1

Reflection

Dear Child of God, the Lord wants you to live a life worthy of your call. Our highest call is to be Christians, people associated with Christ, people belonging to the rank of Christ. We must therefore justify that we belong to the camp of Jesus by acting as He would and making Him visible to others, through our lifestyle and actions.

PRAYER

Lord Jesus, I belong to you. May this be visible enough through the way I live and the choices I make.
Amen.

Day 5

DO NOT BE CONFORMED TO THE WORLD

² Do not be conformed to this world, but be transformed by the renewing of your minds, so that you may discern what is the will of God—what is good and acceptable and perfect.
Romans 12:2

Reflection

Dear Child of God, we are in this world, but we do not belong to this world. Our values, vision, goals, longing, perspective and hopes are different. Let us not be entangled by the pattern of this world. Our standard should not be set by the world, by the preference of majority but by the will of God. It is what God wills and commands that is good, acceptable and perfect, even if society thinks otherwise.

PRAYER

Lord Jesus, may I live in this world not for the world but for you who love and died for me. Amen.

Day 6

ACT FOR THE GOOD OF OTHERS

24 Do not seek your own advantage,
but that of the other.
1 Corinthians 10:24

Reflection

Dear Child of God, in Christ, we learn the example of selflessness. He left His glory to share in our humanity, not for His sake but for our sake. He gave everything for us even His life. In this, He has given us an example. We who are called by His name ought to imitate His example. Let us be motivated by selflessness. Let us act for the good of others and not use them for our own interest or for seeking our own advantage.

PRAYER

Lord Jesus, thank you for giving me an example of complete selflessness. May I practise this in my relationship with others today and always. Amen.

Day 7

THE EXAMPLE OF NOAH

⁹ These are the descendants of Noah. Noah was a righteous man, blameless in his generation; Noah walked with God.
Genesis 6:9

Reflection

Dear Child of God, the example of Noah is set before us today. The Word of God describes Him as a righteous man, blameless in his generation and he walked with God. Keep in mind that Noah lived among rebellious, ungodly and corrupt people but yet he remained upright before God. The Lord needs people like Noah in our generation, people who will not allow themselves to be corrupted by the evil influence around them, people who will walk with God in faithfulness, people who would rather die than wilfully offend the Lord. Can you be one of these people?

PRAYER

Lord Jesus, I want to be like Noah in my generation. I acknowledge that I am weak, and I often fail you, but I rely on your grace and I surrender myself to you.
Amen.

Day 8

SERVE THE LORD THROUGH YOUR WORK

*[23] Whatever your task, put yourselves into it,
as done for the Lord and not for your masters,
[24] since you know that from the Lord you will
receive the inheritance as your reward; you
serve the Lord Christ.*
Colossians 3:23-24

Reflection

Dear Child of God, whatever is your duty, do it joyfully and turn it into service for the Lord. As we work today, we should offer all we do as a thanksgiving to God for the grace to be able to work. We should conscientiously serve the Lord through our daily tasks and look to Him for encouragement and reward. Even if we are not appreciated by others, the Lord sees all we do, and He will reward us.

PRAYER

Lord Jesus, I offer you all I will do today. Let me do it with thanksgiving and with the new delight of serving you.
Amen.

166

Day 9

YOU WILL BE A TREASURED POSSESSION

*5 "Now therefore, if you obey my voice and keep my
covenant, you shall be my treasured possession out
of all the peoples. Indeed, the whole earth is mine,
6 but you shall be for me a priestly kingdom and a
holy nation. These are the words that you shall
speak to the Israelites."*
Exodus 19:5-6

Reflection

The Lord promises to make us his treasured
possession, a priestly kingdom and a holy nation. What
does it mean to be a priestly people? Only the priests
have access to the holy of holies and can present the
sacrifice of the people to God. Dear Child of God, God
promises to extend this privilege to us all and this He
has fulfilled in Christ. We all can now have access to
God, we can stand in the gap between God and others,
we can offer Him a fitting sacrifice of praise and
prayers. As we rejoice in our privilege through Christ,
let us remember that the Lord demands obedience
from us and faithfulness to our promise to Him.

PRAYER

Lord Jesus, you are the eternal high priest. You
have offered yourself as the supreme sacrifice
and given us access to the Father. May I offer to
the Lord also, all that I have and all that I am.
Amen.

THE DISCIPLINE OF THE ALMIGHTY

¹⁷ How happy is the one whom God reproves; therefore do not despise the discipline of the Almighty.
Job 5:17

Reflection

Dear Child of God, as part of our training in righteousness, maturity in faith and in godly character, God sometimes disciplines us. Every parent disciplines their child to make them learn and be responsible. God is the ideal parent. When He disciplines us, it is not out of wickedness or hatred. God is pure love and all His actions proceed from a place of pure love. Let us therefore accept His chastisement in good spirit because He does nothing except for our good.

PRAYER

Lord Jesus, I accept the Father's discipline for my good. Open my eyes to see what is good in what the Father wills, and that I endure for my own sake.
Amen.

Day 11

ILL-GOTTEN TREASURES

² Treasures gained by wickedness do not profit, but righteousness delivers from death. ³ The Lord does not let the righteous go hungry, but He thwarts the craving of the wicked.

Proverbs 10:2-3

Reflection

Dear Child of God, the Lord knows our needs and He is willing to bless us. There is more reward in hard work and honesty than crookedness. Any gain that comes from disobeying God or cheating others is not blessed and the end is regret. Trust in the Lord and not on sinful smartness. The Lord will supply your need and you will never lack.

PRAYER

Lord Jesus, you multiplied bread and fish for those who followed you and you filled them to satisfaction. I trust in your providence and care. Keep my heart from crookedness and deceit. Amen.

GOD LOVES A CHEERFUL GIVER

⁷ Each of you must give as you have made up your mind, not reluctantly or under compulsion, for God loves a cheerful giver.
2 Corinthians 9:7

Reflection

Dear Child of God, we are constantly being looked after by God. He blesses us so that we can bless others. None of us is so poor that he/she has nothing to share with others. Let us always be generous and be willing to share with others from what we have received from God. As we keep asking, let us also be pleased to give and give joyfully and cheerfully, for God loves not just any giver but the one who is joyful in giving and the one who gives with a true smile.

PRAYER

Lord Jesus, you are a joyful giver. Let me imitate your examples by giving joyfully to others.
Amen.

Day 13

SEEK NO EVIL

Seek good, not evil, that you may live. Then the Lord God Almighty will be with you, just as you say He is.

Amos 5:14

Reflection

Dear Child of God, the Lord has promised He will be with you to bless, protect, defend and support you. However, God doesn't defend one who seeks evil and wishes evil to others. He is a good God who supports no evil. To enjoy His loving presence, let us seek good and let us work for the good of others. Let us not initiate, support or promote what is evil in the sight of God.

PRAYER

Lord Jesus, help me to shun evil and seek and strive after what is good for my soul and the wellbeing of others.

Amen.

Day 14

DO NOT SHARE IN ANYONE'S GUILT

[17] You shall not hate in your heart anyone of your kin; you shall reprove your neighbour, or you will incur guilt yourself.

Reflection

There are different ways of sharing in the guilt of the sins of others. One of them is by silence. When you see your friend speaking blasphemy and you laugh and enjoy the joke, you are as guilty as your friend. When you observe injustice and you maintain a safe silence, you are guilty of promoting it. Wisdom is knowing when to be silent and when to speak out.

Dear Child of God, when you observe something is not right, do not be quiet but speak out in charity and with clarity. Never be a part of sin and injustice through silence. Silence doesn't excuse us from guilt.

PRAYER

Lord Jesus, help me to be a voice of truth and give me the courage to speak out against what runs contrary to faith, justice and right reason. Amen.

Day 15

I WILL SERVE THE LORD

15 Now if you are unwilling to serve the Lord,
choose this day whom you will serve, whether the
gods your ancestors served in the region beyond
the River or the gods of the Amorites in whose
land you are living; but as for me and my
household, we will serve the Lord.

Joshua 24:15

Reflection

Joshua openly confessed that He and his household would serve the Lord. He made a decision and was willing to make it openly. Dear Child of God, the question is thrown at you - who do you want to serve? You may answer "but I am serving the Lord already." Think carefully. Often we serve ourselves, we serve our interests, we serve our ego, but we hide this under service to God. The Lord knows those who claim to serve Him but do not and He knows those who really serve Him, those who genuinely love Him and place Him above and beyond every other thing. Are you ready to say like Joshua today, "I will serve the Lord."

PRAYER

Lord Jesus, help me to love and serve you in
spirit and in truth.
Amen.

TO PLEASE GOD IS OUR GOAL

⁴ ... but just as we have been approved by God to be entrusted with the message of the Gospel, even so we speak, not to please mortals, but to please God who tests our hearts. ⁵ As you know and as God is our witness, we never came with words of flattery or with a pretext for greed.

1 Thessalonians 2:4-5

Reflection

St. Paul says we speak not to please mortals, but to please God who tests our hearts. Dear Child of God, the easiest road to frustration is to try to please mortals. Why not channel your energy towards pleasing God and Him alone. Then those who are aiming at pleasing God as well, will be pleased with you. Seeking to please people often becomes an occasion of temptation, a cause of frustration and it distracts us from what pleases God.

PRAYER

Lord Jesus, your mission was to please and glorify your Father. Help me to focus ultimately on this, for when you are pleased with me, it matters not who is displeased.
Amen.

Day 17

LET LOVE BE GENUINE

⁹ Let love be genuine; hate what is evil,
hold fast to what is good
Romans 12:9

Reflection

Our world today is suffering from scarcity of true love. There is an avalanche of lust and pretentious love, but true love is scarce. True love seeks the good of others and not our own interest. True love forgives; it is unconditional and sacrificial. It doesn't rejoice over evil or hold unto grudges. We need more of this to heal our world and to make it a better place. Dear Child of God, true love is what you have experienced in God and this is what we must show to one another.

PRAYER

Lord Jesus, I marvel at your love for me. Help me to transmit genuine love to others and to play my part in making this world a better place. Amen.

Day 18

THE SPIRIT OF DELILAH

18 When Delilah realised that he had told her his whole secret, she sent and called the lords of the Philistines, saying, "This time come up, for he has told his whole secret to me." Then the lords of the Philistines came up to her and brought the money in their hands.

Judges 16:18

Reflection

Delilah lured Samson into trusting her and disclosing his secret to her. When Samson had done this, she quickly divulged it to the enemies of Samson and accepted payment for this betrayal. Dear Child of God, let the spirit of Delilah not reside in you. Do not publicise the secrets of those who confide in you. Do not break people's trust. Do not betray those who hold you as a true friend. Do not allow love of money to tempt you to sin against charity.

PRAYER

Lord Jesus, renew my mind by the power of your spirit. May I love as you have loved me and expunge from me every tendency to betray others.
Amen.

Day 19

TALK TO GOD FIRST

"O Lord, please hear my prayer! Listen to the prayers of those of us who delight in honouring you. Please grant me success today by making the king favourable to me. Put it into his heart to be kind to me." In those days I was the king's cup-bearer.

Nehemiah 1:11

Reflection

Nehemiah was heartbroken because of the state of Jerusalem and the temple. He made up his mind to approach the king to seek permission to go and help to rebuild the temple in Jerusalem. He did not rush to the presence of the king. He knelt before the Lord, and he begged for mercy and favour as he approached the king. The Lord heard his prayer and he found favour before the king. Dear Child of God, what plans do you have today? Who are you going to talk to? Have you first talked to God about it? When you kneel before God, you will be able to stand before anyone. When you find favour before God, it will be easy to find favour before those who matter.

PRAYER

Lord Jesus, I bring before you all I have in mind to do and all those I will approach with any request. Please go before me and may it be well with me.

Amen.

GOD IS THE GIVER OF TRUE JOY

You have put gladness in my heart more than when their grain and wine abound.

Psalm 4:7

Reflection

The Lord is a giver of joy; He makes our lives sweet and meaningful. Many people think that pleasure and joy are in sin. This is the devil blindfolding people and deceiving them away from true joy. Brief is the pleasure of sin; regret is the consequence and eternity is the punishment. Dear Child of God, listen to the Psalmist saying to us that God puts more gladness in our heart than an abundance of grain and new wine; more than any sinful pleasure can ever afford. Let us ask God to open our hearts to receive and taste of His pleasure and we shall want nothing more of sin.

PRAYER

Lord Jesus, those who encounter you encounter joy unspeakable. Fill my heart with new joy and let others see this and seek you, the source of true and lasting joy.
Amen.

Day 21

THE LORD CARES HOW WE TREAT OTHERS

[5] The Lord spoke to Moses, saying: [6] Speak to the Israelites: When a man or a woman wrongs another, breaking faith with the Lord, that person incurs guilt [7] and shall confess the sin that has been committed. The person shall make full restitution for the wrong, adding one-fifth to it, and giving it to the one who was wronged.
Numbers 5:5-7

Reflection

Dear Child of God, the Lord is interested in how we conduct ourselves in His presence, and how we treat other people. When we treat others without fairness or compassion we break faith with the Lord. God demands that we confess such sins and seek pardon from the person we have wronged. Atonement may just be an apology or any act that could repair the damage or help the person heal. Let us try as much as we can, not to intentionally be unkind or unjust to anyone. The golden law is 'do to others as you want them to do to you' or better still, treat others as you want God to treat you.

PRAYER

Lord Jesus, you are immeasurably kind to me. Help me to be fair and kind to others and to be humble enough to confess to you and apologise to those I might have wronged.
Amen.

Day 22

WRONG COUNSEL

¹³ The king answered the people harshly. He disregarded the advice that the older men had given him ¹⁴ and spoke to them according to the advice of the young men, "My father made your yoke heavy, but I will add to your yoke; my father disciplined you with whips, but I will discipline you with scorpions."

1 Kings 12:13-14

Reflection

King Rehoboam, the son of King Solomon, sought advice on how to address his subjects. The older people advised him to promise to be kind to them and to be considerate. The younger ones advised him to instil fear in the subjects, to gain respect by threatening them. This he followed and that was his doom. Dear Child of God, let us be careful about who we go to for advice. Let us be discerning and sensible in the advice we take. Let us beware of the counsel we give people. Anyone who misleads others by foolish counsel will not be spared of guilt.

PRAYER

Lord Jesus, help me to be discerning enough to know and accept what is right before you and to be prudent enough to reject what will lead me to regret.

Amen.

Day 23

LIVE BY THE SPIRIT

*[16] Live by the Spirit, I say, and do not gratify
the desires of the flesh.*
Galatians 5:16

Reflection

There are two kinds of life we can live - life according
to the flesh or life in the Spirit. Life according to the
flesh means to be governed by carnal principles. It is a
pleasure-seeking kind of existence, it is a life of
bondage to sin, a life characterised by sinful habit and
dictatorship of our base desires and appetites, especially
the desire for sexual immorality in all its forms, shades
and expression. To live by the Spirit is to obey a
different law. It is living according to the will of God,
the dictates of His word, living the life of heaven here
on earth. In this life, our appetites, longing and
yearning is for God and all that does Him honour.
Dear Child of God, this is the life we are all called to
live. It is a life of truth, freedom, heavenly peace and
true joy.

PRAYER

Lord Jesus, help me to live my life not according
to the dictates of my flesh but the guidance of
the Spirit.
Amen.

DO NOT GIVE HEED TO EVERYTHING YOU HEAR

²¹ Do not give heed to everything that people say, or you may hear your servant cursing you; ²² your heart knows that many times you have yourself cursed others.
Ecclesiastes 7:21-22

Reflection

Often we are upset and distressed because of what we hear people say about us. Sometimes we lose sleep because someone has told us that someone else has said something derogatory about us. It can be painful when we hear unpleasant comments about us. However, dear Child of God, do not overrate what people are saying about you, do not base your life on public opinion. The fact that people are praising you doesn't mean God is praising you and the fact that people are talking ill about you doesn't mean God is unhappy with you. Pay less attention to what is said about you. Seek to do your best and to please God. Be careful what you also say about others too. It would be unjust to say unpleasant things about others and be angry when we hear such things said about us.

PRAYER

Lord Jesus, help me to be careful what I say about others and not to overrate what people say or think about me. Let me keep in mind that in the long run, what you say is what is paramount. Amen.

Day 25

THE SIN OF CONFORMITY

*¹The Lord spoke to Moses, saying: ²Speak to
the people of Israel and say to them: I am the
Lord your God. ³ You shall not do as they do
in the land of Egypt, where you lived, and
you shall not do as they do in the land of
Canaan, to which I am bringing you. You
shall not follow their statutes.*
Leviticus 18:1-3

Reflection

Speaking through Moses, God warned the people of
Israel not to copy the lifestyle, values, statutes and
practices of the Egyptians and the Canaanites. Dear
Child of God, the Lord warns us today against the sin
of conformity. We must be careful not to imitate any
custom, habit, value or lifestyle of those who are
essentially worldly. We must not try to be like those
who do not care about God or faith. We should not
discriminate against them, but we should remember
we are different.

PRAYER

Lord Jesus, help me to remain uncompromising
in my faith and values. May I not conform
myself to the pattern of worldly people.
Amen.

Day 26

PUT NO STUMBLING BLOCK

[13] Let us therefore no longer pass judgment on one another but resolve instead never to put a stumbling block or hindrance in the way of another.
Romans 14:13

Reflection

Dear Child of God, the Lord invites you today to make a resolution; the resolution never to put a stumbling block in the way of another. This means that we should not become an occasion of sin to another, we should not be the reason why someone's walk with God will be difficult, we must not make it difficult for someone to live a holy life, either by tempting them or discouraging them. Let us seek to lead people to God and not away from Him.

PRAYER

Lord Jesus, make me a light in the world and not a cause of darkness. May I lead people to you and not away from your love.
Amen.

Day 27

HANNAH BROUGHT HER PAINS TO GOD

¹⁰She was deeply distressed and prayed to the Lord and wept bitterly. ¹¹She made this vow: "O Lord of hosts, if only you will look on the misery of your servant, and remember me, and not forget your servant, but will give to your servant a male child, then I will set him before you as a nazirite until the day of his death. He shall drink neither wine nor intoxicants, and no razor shall touch his head."

1 Samuel 1:10-11

Reflection

Hannah was sad and deeply distressed because of her delay in child birth and the mockery she endured in the hands of Peninnah. She decided to bring her pains and sorrow to the Lord. She wept bitterly, prayed to the Lord and made a vow before the Lord. Dear Child of God, when you are distressed or troubled in spirit, do not say "I do not even feel like praying." Do not allow your needs to create a distance between you and God. Instead, take them to the Lord in prayers. He is not unmoved by our tears and sorrow.

PRAYER

Lord Jesus, thank you for the comfort of knowing that I can cast my burdens to you. May I never bear alone what I can bring before you. Amen.

PONDER ON GOD'S WORD

⁸ This book of the law shall not depart out of your mouth; you shall meditate on it day and night, so that you may be careful to act in accordance with all that is written in it. For then you shall make your way prosperous, and then you shall be successful.

Joshua 1:8

Reflection

Joshua was told the secret of wisdom and success. He should speak upon himself the words of the law of God, ponder on it day and night and carefully act in accordance with all that is written in it. Dear Child of God, do you need the password to access the store of wisdom and success? You need not go far. Grab your Bible and meditate on it by day and night. Speak out what it contains and live according to what it teaches. Your life will be beautiful, fruitful and meaningful.

PRAYER

Lord Jesus, your Word is life. May I grow in wisdom and fruitfulness as I examine your Word.
Amen.

Day 29

IT IS NOT USELESS TO SERVE THE LORD

18 Then once more you shall see the difference between the righteous and the wicked, between one who serves God and one who does not serve Him.
Malachi 3:18

Reflection

The people of Israel say it is useless to serve the Lord because those who do not serve the Lord seem to be more prosperous and happy. They have less trouble and they sin and go scot free. God replied that soon they would see that it pays to serve the Lord when they see the punishment that awaits the unrighteous and what God has in store for those who live rightly. Dear Child of God, maybe you are thinking this way, or you may one day be faced with these thoughts. Remember that there is great gain and blessing in serving God. The greatest gain is heaven which is not a place for the ungodly.

PRAYER

Lord Jesus, I know that serving you is gain and rewarding. Save me from stumbling and comparing my lot with those of others, for your plan for me is good and cannot be seen through the lens of others.
Amen.

Day 30

FEAR GOD, RESPECT PEOPLE

[7] And after a time his master's wife cast her eyes on Joseph and said, "Lie with me." [8] But he refused and said to his master's wife, "Look, with me here, my master has no concern about anything in the house, and he has put everything that he has in my hand. [9] He is not greater in this house than I am, nor has he kept back anything from me except yourself, because you are his wife. How then could I do this great wickedness, and sin against God?"

Genesis 39:7-9

Reflection

The wife of Potiphar saw Joseph and wanted to lure him to bed with her, but Joseph refused, even though she was powerful, and he respected her. Joseph recognised that it is a great respect to those we love, to refuse to oblige them when they want to come between us and God's command. Joseph did not give in to her sinful advances because he feared God, and human respect would not make him undermine God. Dear Child of God, when we love or respect people so much that we can't say no to them when they want us to offend God, we no longer respect but we are worshipping them. They have become gods in our lives, and we should have no other God than the Lord.

PRAYER

Lord Jesus, help me to resist every temptation to offend your love for me. May human respect not rob me of reverence and love for you. Amen.

188

JULY

Day 1

AMBASSADOR OF GOD

²⁰for which I am an ambassador in chains.
Pray that I may declare it boldly,
as I must speak.
Ephesians 6:20

Reflection

Dear Child of God, wherever you are, in whatever circumstances you find yourself, do not forget your identity - you are an ambassador of God. You are to make God known, loved, cherished and served. People must see the goodness of God in you and hear you proclaim His greatness. Do not go crying or telling others how miserable your life is. Do not give the impression that your God is unfair to you. Even in chains, St. Paul still spoke of God's gracious love and goodness, because His goodness endures forever and in all circumstances.

PRAYER

Lord Jesus, make me a good ambassador in the world. May I present to others a true image of your love.
Amen.

Day 2
DO WHAT IS RIGHT ALWAYS

⁶not only while being watched, and in order to please them, but as slaves of Christ, doing the will of God from the heart.

Ephesians 6:6

Reflection

Dear Child of God, let us learn to do what is right and lawful, whether we are under supervision or not. Let our motivation for doing what is right not be to escape punishment or to please people but rather because we are our watch and our conscience is our supervisor. Whether we are seen or not, let us be responsible.

PRAYER

Lord Jesus, you see everything, and you know everything. Help me to act rightly and justly, not to escape chastisement or please anyone but to please you, my Lord.
Amen.

Day 3

SPIRITUAL WARFARE

¹² For our struggle is not against enemies of blood and flesh, but against the rulers, against the authorities, against the cosmic powers of this present darkness, against the spiritual forces of evil in the heavenly places.

Ephesians 6:12

Reflection

Dear Child of God, St. Paul reminds us of something very important today. As long as we are in this world, we are in spiritual warfare. Often we focus on the wrong battle and fight the wrong people. We are being reminded that we are waging war against a spiritual army under the headship of Satan. The goal of our spiritual enemies is to knock us down from our place of standing. To be ignorant or ignore this fact will lead to our loss. Let us, therefore, put on the full armour of God and fight as champions because Christ has already claimed victory for us.

PRAYER

Lord Jesus, you have already conquered for me on the cross. Help me to fight gallantly under your command and claim the victory which was already won for me on the cross.
Amen.

192

Day 4

SEEK PEACE

*¹⁹ Let us then pursue what makes for peace
and for mutual upbuilding.*
Romans 14:19

Reflection

Dear Child of God, the Lord wants us to seek and strive for what will bring about peace and mutual upbuilding. Accusing one another, looking for the fault and downfall of one another, speaking ill about others, encouraging gossip and backbiting, spreading a false rumour about others will not bring peace and is not healthy for the growth of a community. May we learn to shun the things that could divide us and go after the things that could strengthen our bond of love and unity.

PRAYER

Lord Jesus, help us to preserve the gift of unity you have given us, by avoiding what threatens it and investing in what will promote it.
Amen.

SEEK THE WELLBEING OF OTHERS

²Each of us must please our neighbour for the good purpose of building up the neighbour.
Romans 15:2

Reflection

Dear Child of God, the Lord wants us to seek not just our gains but the joy and wellbeing of others. We are reminded today to put others into consideration in our decisions and actions. Let us do what pleases not just ourselves but what can bring joy to our neighbours and build them up.

PRAYER

Lord Jesus, help me to seek not just my good but the good and wellbeing of others.
Amen.

Day 6

QUALITIES OF LOVE

⁴ Love is patient; love is kind; love is not envious or boastful or arrogant ⁵ or rude. It does not insist on its own way; it is not irritable or resentful; ⁶ it does not rejoice in wrongdoing but rejoices in the truth.

1 Corinthians 13:4-6

Reflection

Dear Child of God, St. Paul gives us here the qualities of love. These qualities are perfected in God because God is love. We are called to be like God through love. The extent of our love is the extent of our Christian maturity. Let me propose a test for us. Where we have the word "love is...", let us replace love by putting our names and see if it fits. This is a good way to test our maturity in godliness.

PRAYER

Lord Jesus, you are love itself. Help me to love truly and to discover a vocation in loving others.
Amen.

I WILL BE A FATHER TO YOU

*⁸and I will be your father, and you shall be
my sons and daughters, says the Lord
Almighty.*

2 Corinthians 6:18

Reflection

Dear Child of God, we are reminded today of God's promise to us. He promises to be gracious to us, to be a Father to us and to accept us as His sons and daughters. Let us live this day in the consciousness that God is our dad. Our dad is also our friend. He is there at our side, to lead, guide and watch over us. We are not orphans and helpless, we are not miserable and destitute. The King of the universe has adopted us, and He loves us in a way that is personal, intimate and profound.

PRAYER

Lord Jesus, thank you for opening the gate for us to be welcomed into God's household. May we be constantly reminded of who we are - sons and daughters of the all-powerful God.
Amen.

Day 8

I WON'T LEAVE YOU AS ORPHANS

¹⁸I will not leave you orphaned; I am coming to you.

John 14:18

Reflection

Dear Child of God, Jesus has given us His word. He says He won't leave us helpless, without protection, provision or instruction. This promise holds true today. The Holy Spirit has been given to be our helper. Let us keep this in mind and ask the help of the Holy Spirit when we need support, instruction and assistance. All we need to live life to the full has been supplied to us in Jesus, through the power of the Holy Spirit.

PRAYER

Lord Jesus, thank you for your promise. Whenever I feel helpless and alone, in need and unsafe, may I keep in mind that I am not an orphan, that you are alive and with me through the Holy Spirit and all I need shall be supplied from above.

Amen.

YOU REAP WHAT YOU SOW

⁷Do not be deceived; God is not mocked, for
you reap whatever you sow.
Galatians 6:7

Reflection

Dear Child of God, it is very easy to fool and deceive others, but God cannot be deceived. No one can pretend before Him, lie to Him or escape His eyes. He sees, knows and rewards all things. Whatever we sow is what we reap. With this consciousness, let us be sincere with Him and serve Him faithfully. Let us generously sow the seed of love, justice, peace and kindness, so that we may with joy reap bountifully in time and eternal harvest.

PRAYER

Lord Jesus, help me through the power of the Holy Spirit to multiply good works, so that I may reap good fruits in eternal harvest.
Amen.

Day 10

DO NOT RUSH TO ACT

²Desire without knowledge is not good, and one who moves too hurriedly misses the way.

Proverbs 19:2

Reflection

Dear Child of God, the Lord wants us to always reflect carefully, to exercise greater patience and pray before we act or decide on something. Often we rush to act, respond or make a decision and then we discover we are wrong, and we have made mistakes. Try not to be hasty today; reflect on what you want to do or say, pray about it, ask the Lord to direct you to do what is most proper and free you from dangerous mistakes.

PRAYER

Lord Jesus, order my steps today and direct my affairs. Teach me to slow down when I need to slow and to think rightly before acting.
Amen.

Day 11

WALK AS A WISE PERSON

15 But speaking the truth in love, we must grow up in every way into Him who is the head, into Christ

Ephesians 4:15

Reflection

Dear Child of God, reflect on the counsel of St. Paul today. Look carefully then how you walk, not as unwise but as wise. An unwise person pursues pleasure that can ruin his/her soul. An unwise person doesn't think about God and others before making a decision. An unwise person seeks the ruin of others. An unwise person wastes time and forgets that no condition is permanent. An unwise person does not think about his end and judgement. Let us not live like unwise but wise persons.

PRAYER

Lord Jesus, help me to live each day in the wisdom of the Holy Spirit. May I not live foolishly but sensibly.

Amen.

Day 12

YOUR SPECIAL PLACE IN GOD'S FAMILY

[19] So then you are no longer strangers and aliens, but you are citizens with the saints and also members of the household of God

Ephesians 2:19

Reflection

Dear Child of God, we are reminded of our special place in the family of God's people. We are no longer strangers and sojourners, but we are fellow citizens with the saints and important members of the household of God. While on earth, we belong to a human family which quite often is characterised by problems. Many of us are unhappy because our family is messed up. We are reminded today that even though there is no perfect family on earth, we belong to a perfect family, the family of God's people and we are very important in this family. The angels and saints are our relatives and Jesus is our eldest brother, the first born from the dead.

PRAYER

Lord Jesus, thanking you for making us a member of your household. May we conduct ourselves as members of a holy, royal and perfect family.
Amen.

Day 13

BE CAREFUL OF EMPTY DECEIT

⁸See to it that no one takes you captive through philosophy and empty deceit, according to human tradition, according to the elemental spirits of the universe, and not according to Christ.
Colossians 2:8

Reflection

There are many people in our world today trying hard to discredit our Christian faith and practises by their complex argument and demonic logic. There are so many ideas, opinions and thesis aimed at negating the truths of faith and sowing the seed of doubt and confusion in people. As for you dear Child of God, be careful of these thoughts, these philosophies and empty deceit. They are engineered by the elemental spirit of this world. They are at the service of the devil, the father of confusion. Hold fast to the truth as contained in the Word of God and accurately taught in the Church of Christ. Do not open your heart to error and deception.

PRAYER

Lord Jesus, help me to identify and reject whatever is false and misleading, no matter how logical and convincing it may appear to be. Amen.

Day 14

LET THE WORD OF GOD DWELL RICHLY IN YOU

*¹⁶ Let the word of Christ dwell in you richly;
teach and admonish one another in all
wisdom; and with gratitude in your hearts
sing psalms, hymns, and spiritual songs to
God.*
Colossians 3:16

Reflection

Just as the Word became flesh and dwelt among us, the Word of God wants to also become flesh in our hearts. The Lord wants us to open our hearts for another incarnation to take place. This time around, it is in our hearts. The Word of God is not just to dwell in our head as one who memorises it or on our mouth as one who merely quotes. It must dwell in our heart as one who listens, studies, ponders on it and integrates it into his/her life and bears fruits of good works through the Word.

PRAYER

Lord Jesus, may your Word dwell in my heart and bear fruit of good works and righteousness. Amen.

DO NOT BE TIRED OF DOING GOOD

¹³ Brothers and sisters, do not be weary in doing what is right.

2 Thessalonians 3:13

Reflection

Dear Child of God, a time comes when we tend to get tired of things. We tend to get tired of what we do, maybe where we live, something that we once loved, a place we once loved to visit, a game we once loved to play, a song we once loved to hear, a company we once loved to keep, an activity we once delighted in. Today, the Lord is telling us, we may be tired of these things, places and events but there is something you must never be tired of - that is, doing good.

PRAYER

Lord Jesus, you went about doing good and you were never tired or discouraged. May I never be tired of doing good and may I never allow myself to be discouraged.
Amen.

Day 16

BE NOT HASTY TO BELIEVE

19 When his master heard the words that his wife spoke to him, saying, "This is the way your servant treated me," he became enraged. 20 And Joseph's master took him and put him into the prison, the place where the king's prisoners were confined; he remained there in prison.
Genesis 39:19-20

Reflection

Dear Child of God, do not be hasty to believe what you hear about others. Do not make a judgement without careful investigation. Do not condemn anyone based on the account of another person. Be quick to listen, be slow to judge and speak. People exaggerate and embellish stories, people lie a lot, people invent episodes to tarnish those they do not like. Sometimes people give us a single narrative to drag us into hating those they hate. Potiphar's wife lied to him and because of this an innocent man was put in prison and the one who should have been in the prison enjoyed full but false liberty. This is not uncommon in our world today. May the Lord save us from condemning the innocent.

PRAYER

Lord Jesus, teach me to be slow to judge and not to be too quick to believe but give me the spirit of discernment and wisdom to perceive beyond what I am told to what is true.
Amen.

PREPARE YOURSELF

*⁴So Moses went down from the mountain
to the people. He consecrated the people,
and they washed their clothes.*

Exodus 19:14

Reflection

Moses consecrated the people and they washed their garments because they were preparing to meet with the Lord. Whenever we want to come before the Lord in worship, to receive Him in Communion or approach Him in prayer, He wants us to prepare ourselves, to wash our garment from spot and stains of sins. God is holy and holiness in the lives of those who approach Him is pleasing to Him. Let us be careful not to come before the Lord with a garment stained and soiled by iniquities. The blood of Jesus washes garments clean more than any detergent, and this is applied to our souls when we come to the sacrament of reconciliation.

PRAYER

Lord Jesus, I come before you this day. Wash me thoroughly from my iniquity and cleanse me from my sins.
Amen.

Day 18

DO NOT STEAL

¹⁵ *You shall not steal.*

Exodus 20:15

Reflection

Dear Child of God, the devil is a thief and a murderer. As for you, let none of these tendencies be found in you - theft or murderous spirit. Steer clear of anything that has the appearance of theft. Do not keep for your use whatever is not yours. Do not cheat others or rob them of what is theirs. Do not desire to possess what belongs to another person. Do not borrow without the intention of returning and do not delay returning what you have borrowed. Do not hoard what should be given out in charity and do not multiply your gains through dubious means. When we increase our resources and possessions by theft or other ungodly means, we block ourselves from God's blessings.

PRAYER

Lord Jesus, let me always be honest and true to my neighbours and in my life. Help me to live my life in charity.
Amen.

Day 19

AGAINST COVETOUSNESS

*17You shall not covet your neighbour's
house; you shall not covet your neighbour's
wife, or male or female slave, or ox, or
donkey, or anything that belongs to your
neighbour.*
Exodus 20:17

Reflection

Dear Child of God, God gives to each of us according
to His will and according to what is good and necessary
for us. The Lord doesn't withhold from any of us
whatever is necessary for us to live the life He wants us
to live. He doesn't deny us what is important for our
salvation. However, it is not everything we desire that
will come to us. This is where we must learn
contentment and avoid envy, greed and covetousness.
Do not seek to acquire, possess or rob your neighbours
of what God has been pleased to give them. If God
thinks you should have it, He will give it to you. Do
not be unkind or mean to your neighbour because of
what God has done for them.

PRAYER

Lord Jesus, teach me contentment and may
envy of others not make me an ingrate.
Amen.

Day 20

HONOURING OUR PARENTS

³You shall each revere your mother and father, and you shall keep my sabbaths: I am the Lord your God.

Leviticus 19:3

Reflection

Dear Child of God, reverence to our parents is very important. No matter how weak, poor or uneducated they are, no matter what they may have done wrong to us, the Lord says we must honour and not dishonour them. Part of honouring them is to respect them, forgive them, take care of them. For those who do not know Christ, we should help them to know the Lord. We should make them proud of us by not ruining but honouring our family name. This same love and reverence extends also to our godparents, guardians and all those who act as parents and teachers to us.

PRAYER

Lord Jesus, help me to honour my parents and all those whom you have used to help me to become who you want me to become in life. Grant eternal rest to the departed and your grace to the living.

Amen.

Day 21

GOD'S BREATH IS IN YOU

*⁴The spirit of God has made me, and the
breath of the Almighty gives me life.*

Job 33:4

Reflection

Dear Child of God, you are not an accident in the
world, you are a portion of God, you are divine. How?
God's Spirit is in you, the breath of the Almighty is in
you. That is, you are the bearer of God's breath. This
implies so many things. It reminds us that we are from
God and that we are nothing without God. This is why
when we separate or distance ourselves from God, we
separate and distance ourselves from the source of life
in us. This is nothing but spiritual death.

PRAYER

Lord Jesus, I acknowledge that God's breath is
what keeps me alive. May I never separate
myself from the source of my being.
Amen.

Day 22

AGREE WITH GOD

[21] Agree with God and be at peace; in this way good will come to you.

Job 22:21

Reflection

Sometimes we argue with God, we contend with His will for us, we disagree with His word, we insist on our way, we are impatient with His plan, we refuse to respond to His call and bow to His discipline. When we are in this state of disagreement with God, we lose our peace, we face the road that leads to emptiness and depression, hopelessness and sadness. Dear Child of God, here is a powerful counsel for us: "Agree with God and be at peace; thereby good will come to you."

PRAYER

Lord Jesus, in your will is my peace. I surrender to you and accept your plans for my life. Amen.

CALL ON ME IN TROUBLE

*[15]Call on me in the day of trouble; I will
deliver you, and you shall glorify me.*
Psalm 50:15

Reflection

Dear Child of God, what do you do on days of trouble?
Do you cry endlessly? Do you run helter-skelter? Do
you place your hope on people to be your saviour? Do
you compromise your faith, integrity and godly
principles to be out of trouble? The Lord gives you a
solution whenever you are assailed by problems and
troubles. He says you should call on Him and He will
deliver you and you will have cause to glorify Him.
The same way you call ambulance, police or fire service
when things go wrong, you can also dial God's line
when you are weighed down. Simply dial 1+1+1 P-
R-A-Y-E-R.

PRAYER

Lord Jesus, give me the faith to see in you the
solution to all my troubles and worries.
Amen.

Day 24

YOUR SOUL SHOULD NOT BE DOWNCAST

*⁵Why are you cast down, O my soul, and
why are you disquieted within me? Hope in
God; for I shall again praise Him, my help.*

Psalm 42:5

Reflection

Dear Child of God, do not permit your soul to be
downcast. Do not allow it to groan within you. Do not
allow your spirit to stop hoping and your mouth to
stop praising. Whenever you are on that path of sorrow
and self-pity, ginger your soul. Let it begin to praise
God. Praising God liberates us from self-pity, it
enlivens our souls, it gladdens our heart, revives our
spirit, renews our hope, it attracts divine attention and
changes our situation for the better.

PRAYER

Lord Jesus, help me to find new strength, new
joy, new encouragement through praising you.
Amen.

MAY MY WORDS BE ACCEPTABLE

¹⁴Let the words of my mouth and the meditation of my heart be acceptable to you, O Lord, my rock and my redeemer.

Psalm 19:14

Reflection

The Psalmist prays that His words and meditations may be acceptable before God. This is a powerful prayer that we all need to pray - that our words be pleasing to God and the meditation of our heart be acceptable in His sight. However, dear Child of God, it is not enough to pray this. For our words and meditations to be acceptable, our lives must first be acceptable before God. We must be careful to live according to God's will and pleasure. We must learn to surrender to the power and direction of the Holy Spirit. He will sanctify our words and thoughts and make them a sweet fragrance before God.

PRAYER

Lord Jesus, I surrender to the sanctifying work of your Spirit. May your Spirit make holy my thoughts, words and actions.
Amen.

Day 26

LOVE LIKE A MORNING CLOUD

*⁴What shall I do with you, O
Ephraim? What shall I do with you, O
Judah? Your love is like a morning
cloud, like the dew that goes away early.*

Hosea 6:4

Reflection

The Lord described the love of His people like a
morning cloud, like the dew that goes early away. This
means their love is unreliable, inconsistent and
unstable. Dear Child of God, is this how your love for
God is? Do you love Him only when you need
something from Him and breeze away when you have
got what you need? Do you love Him when you are
satisfied and abandon Him when you are in need? The
Lord's love for us is steadfast, constant and unfailing.
He wants us to love Him with constancy too. A love
that is inflated or deflated according to mood, need and
feeling is not what God deserves from us.

PRAYER

Lord Jesus, your love for me is constant and
absolute. Help me to love you as you deserve in
a way that is constant and enduring.
Amen.

DO NOT BE DISTRACTED BY BLESSING

*Israel is a luxuriant vine that yields its fruit.
The more his fruit increased the more altars
he built; as his country improved, he
improved his pillars.*
Hosea 10:1

Reflection

The Lord compared Israel to a luxuriant vine that yields its fruits. Sadly, the more Israel was blessed, the more he abandoned God and followed the desires of his heart. Dear Child of God, our blessing should never turn our backs against God. We should not be as those who got what they wanted from God and allowed their blessing to be an obstacle to serving God. Many ask God for favours and when they receive the favour, they allow it to come between them and God. Let this not be the case with you. Let everything you have received endear you more to the good giver of all gifts.

PRAYER

Lord Jesus, in abundance or scarcity, in riches or poverty, may I serve you joyfully and graciously.
Amen.

Day 28

GOD DOESN'T CHANGE

*⁶For I the Lord do not change; therefore
you, O children of Jacob, have not perished.*
Malachi 3:6

Reflection

Often people who are hitherto kind to us, may
suddenly change without any identifiable reason. Our
friends today can become enemies tomorrow. Those
working for us and with us, may turn tomorrow to
work against us. Those hailing us today may blame us
tomorrow. People change and are unpredictable. Dear
Child of God, God never changes. From everlasting to
everlasting, He is ever the same. He will not grow
older, His character doesn't change. His love for us
doesn't change, His promises and words do not
change. His power doesn't suffer decline and His glory
never fades.

PRAYER

Lord Jesus, thank you for the constancy of your
Word and promise. May I never change my
heart from obeying them and following you
faithfully.
Amen.

Day 29

FOUNTAIN OF MERCY

On that day a fountain shall be opened for the house of David and the inhabitants of Jerusalem, to cleanse them from sin and impurity.
Zechariah 13:1

Reflection

The Lord promised to open for His people a fountain to cleanse them from all uncleanness. This promise is fully fulfilled in Jesus. In Him the fountain of mercy has been opened for the whole world. The blood and water which gushed forth from His side is an exhaustive fount of mercy for those who will approach Him. Dear Child of God, there is no excuse to live in guilt, in sin and in bondage when God has opened for us an ocean of mercy. His mercy is greater than what we have done, what we are doing and what we could ever do, and it is open to whosoever wills.

PRAYER

Lord Jesus, you are the unfathomable Divine Mercy. Envelop the whole world and empty yourself out upon us, that every creature may experience the power of your mercy.
Amen.

Day 30

BE BOLD TO ASK

Ask rain from the Lord in the season of the spring rain, from the Lord who makes the storm clouds, who gives showers of rain to you, the vegetation in the field to everyone.
Zechariah 10:1

Reflection

Ancient Israel had no irrigation system and relied on rain to water their crops. In a time of drought, nothing grew, so Israel relied on both the former rain and the latter rain. The Lord challenged His people saying, be bold enough to ask Me, and I will answer your prayer. I will provide what I alone can provide. The challenge is thrown to you dear Child of God - the Lord wants you to be bold enough, to have the boldness of faith to ask Him for your needs. Nothing is hard for Him. Let us approach Him with confidence, with humility that relies not on merit, with the faith that surrenders to His will. He will not deny us what is good for us.

PRAYER

Lord Jesus, I come to you today. Send your rain to revive my Spirit, rekindle my faith and renew my hope in you.
Amen.

THE LORD IS ON THE THRONE

*In the year that King Uzziah died, I saw
the Lord sitting on a throne, high and lofty;
and the hem of His robe filled the temple.*
Isaiah 6:1

Reflection

In the year that a very powerful and respected king died tragically, a time of mourning and uncertainty, a time that people asked questions and turned to heaven for an answer, Isaiah saw a vision and what did He see? He saw God on the throne. This is very powerful. Kings and rulers, powerful men and women may come and go but God remains on the throne. There may be calamity and distress, disaster and crises but God remains on the throne. To be on the throne means all power, sovereignty and control belongs to Him.

Dear Child of God, whatever your condition and situation is today, just remember that God is on the throne and the one on the throne is in control.

PRAYER

Lord Jesus, I acknowledge that you hold the whole world in your hand and although things may look out of my control, they are never out of your control.
Amen.

AUGUST

Day 1

BE AWAKE

*⁶ So then let us not fall asleep as others do
but let us keep awake and be sober.*
1 Thessalonians 5:6

Reflection

Dear Child of God, we must constantly be spiritually awake and careful, keeping alert and watchful. The enemy watches for a moment when we become too relaxed and careless to bring us down. In the parable of Jesus, the enemy sowed bad seed when the master and labourers were asleep. The price of eternal liberty is eternal vigilance.

PRAYER

Lord Jesus, help me to keep awake spiritually. May I not fall asleep and be robbed by the enemy.
Amen.

Day 2

YOUR LIGHT WILL RISE IN DARKNESS

*⁹Then you shall call, and the Lord will answer; you
shall cry for help, and He will say, Here I am. If you
remove the yoke from among you, the pointing of the
finger, the speaking of evil, ¹⁰if you offer your food to
the hungry and satisfy the needs of the afflicted, then
your light shall rise in the darkness and your gloom
be like the noonday.*
Isaiah 58:9-10

Reflection

The Lord promises to make our light rise in the
darkness and our gloom be as the noon day, but He
expects some things of us. We must not make life
miserable for others by placing any yoke on them. We
must stop pointing accusing fingers and speaking
wickedness. Dear Child of God, we can be a bit more
charitable, a bit more tolerant and forgiving, we can
step aside from unmitigated anger against someone
and then the grace of grace will flow more freely in our
lives.

PRAYER

Lord Jesus, take away from me every sentiment
and action that may dim the light of your glory
in me.
Amen.

Day 3

WE LIVE FOR HIM

¹⁵ And He died for all, so that those who live might live no longer for themselves, but for Him who died and was raised for them.
2 Corinthians 5:15

Reflection

Dear Child of God, remember that Jesus died for us and by His blood, He has paid our ransom. We now belong to Him, we live for Him and for His glory. We have been rescued from the power and bondage of sin, Satan and the flesh. Let us not live as if we live for ourselves and our pleasures alone. Let us live each day in gratitude to Him and for Him who died and rose again for us.

PRAYER

Lord Jesus, by your blood, you have redeemed me. May I live my life for you and may my death glorify you.
Amen.

Day 4

CONSIDER HOW YOU HAVE FARED

⁷Thus says the Lord of hosts: Consider how you have fared. ⁸Go up to the hills and bring wood and build the house, so that I may take pleasure in it and be honoured, says the Lord. ⁹You have looked for much, and, lo, it came to little; and when you brought it home, I blew it away. Why? says the Lord of hosts. Because my house lies in ruins, while all of you hurry off to your own houses.

Haggai 1:7-9

Reflection

The Lord called His people to reflect on how they had fared. They worked so hard but had nothing to show for it. The Lord revealed to them the cause of their problem. They abandoned the project of reconstructing God's temple and focused on their own agenda. The Lord therefore withheld His blessing from what they were doing because they left what He wanted them to prioritise. Dear Child of God, are you working at what God wants you to work at or are you doing your own business? Are you where God wants you to be or are you where you choose to be? One of the causes of stagnation in life is when we are working hard but not according to divine purpose.

PRAYER

Lord Jesus, help me to understand what you want of me at every point so that I don't waste my effort toiling in the wrong direction. Amen.

LAZINESS

₉How long will you lie there, O lazybones? When will you rise from your sleep? ¹⁰A little sleep, a little slumber, a little folding of the hands to rest, ¹¹ and poverty will come upon you like a robber, and want, like an armed warrior.

Proverbs 6:9-11

Reflection

Laziness is a vice we must try to keep away from us. One of the lessons for us from the life of Jesus is how He worked so hard and yet still had time to be alone with the Father in prayer. Dear Child of God, it is not enough for you to pray and fast for breakthrough when you allow idleness and laziness in your life. Prayers, creativity, vision and hard work are important for success in life. Often breakthrough comes in the form of opportunity, but we must be ready for it. Guard against excessive sleeping and time wastage if you want to achieve much in life.

PRAYER

Lord Jesus, your time on earth was short but very productive. Help me to use my time productively and save me from every form of laziness.
Amen.

Day 6

THE LORD IS WITH YOU

¹³ Gideon answered him, "But sir, if the Lord is with us, why then has all this happened to us? And where are all His wonderful deeds that our ancestors recounted to us, saying, 'Did not the Lord bring us up from Egypt?' But now the Lord has cast us off and given us into the hand of Midian."

Judges 6:13

Reflection

The angel of the Lord appeared to Gideon and greeted him with a word of reminder that the Lord was with him. To this, he objected that if the Lord was with them, why was their state so miserable that the Midianites had oppressed them so mercilessly? Dear Child of God, the Lord is not far from any of us. The Lord is always with us. You may be going through a tough time asking the Lord "where are you?" He will simply answer you, "I am here with you, we are in this together." The real challenge is not whether the Lord is with us, it is whether we are with the Lord.

PRAYER

Lord Jesus, I acknowledge that you are always with me. Help me to always be with you as well. Amen.

YOU ARE THE POTTER, I AM THE CLAY

⁶Can I not do with you, O house of Israel,
just as this potter has done? says the Lord.
Just like the clay in the potter's hand, so are
you in my hand, O house of Israel.
Jeremiah 18:6

Reflection

Dear Child of God, we are reminded today that God is like a potter and we are the clay. If we surrender ourselves, He will mould us into a beautiful image, into vessels of honour, the delight of every eye and the pride of the moulder. All He wants from us in order to bring the best out of us is for us to surrender to Him.

PRAYER

Lord Jesus, I surrender to you. Mould me into a vessel of honour, a masterpiece to the glory of your name.
Amen.

Day 8

LORD, SEND SOMEONE ELSE

13 But he said, "O my Lord, please send someone else." 14
Then the anger of the Lord was kindled against Moses and
he said, "What of your brother Aaron the Levite? I know
that he can speak fluently; even now he is coming out to
meet you, and when he sees you his heart will be glad.
Exodus 4:13-14

Reflection

Moses had been praying for the liberation of His people. When the time came which the Lord had ordained to deliver them, He chose Moses as His instrument, but Moses was trying so hard to excuse Himself. He desperately wanted God to deliver them, but He didn't want to be the one to be used for that purpose. Dear Child of God, how often do we give God excuses when He wants to use us for His purpose? Don't we act like Moses sometimes? We want God to usher in a new era, to do something marvellous, to perform a miracle but we are unwilling to be the agent. Today, let us change our perspective, let us quit the habit of always giving God excuses. Let us learn to say "Lord, use me as you will, send me and I will go, if you choose me as the agent of the transformation I am praying for, I will obey."

PRAYER

Lord Jesus, send me to wherever you want, and I will go, speak to me and I will obey. Let whatever you will be my will.
Amen.

Day 9

AN IMPERISHABLE INHERITANCE

³ Blessed be the God and Father of our Lord Jesus Christ! By his great mercy he has given us a new birth into a living hope through the resurrection of Jesus Christ from the dead, ⁴ and into an inheritance that is imperishable, undefiled, and unfading, kept in heaven for you...

1 Peter 1:3-4

Reflection

Dear Child of God, you may not be very rich materially in this world, but you are really blessed and eternally rich. You have a rich and invaluable inheritance kept for you in heaven, which is imperishable, undefiled and unfading. Jesus got this for you through His death and resurrection. He has included you in His will and given you a share of His rich bounty. With this joyful hope, let us look forward to that day when we shall obtain what is ours. As we press forward to that, let us avoid anything that can deprive us of our rich eternal inheritance.

PRAYER

Lord Jesus, thank you for giving me a share of your riches. May I never short change my eternal inheritance for temporal pleasure. Amen.

230

Day 10

IT'S NOT ALL ABOUT MONEY

[16] But he said, "As the Lord lives, whom I serve, I will accept nothing!" He urged him to accept, but he refused.

2 Kings 5:16

Reflection

Naaman urged the prophet Elisha to accept a gift from Him in gratitude for his cure from leprosy but Elisha refused. The gift was attractive, but the man of God was not motivated by greed or tempted by avarice. Dear Child of God, we must not do everything for money or always seek reward or recompense for what we do. Our gain for good work doesn't have to be money. Avarice and greed ruin the divine reward of a good deed. Let us look more to heaven for reward than we look to people's hands and pockets. The first reward of kindness should be the joy of being able to make someone else happy.

PRAYER

Lord Jesus, free my mind from love of money and material things. May I look to you for blessing and reward for the good you have empowered me to do.

Amen.

DO NOT THINK TOO HIGHLY OF YOURSELF

³ For by the grace given to me I say to everyone among you not to think of yourself more highly than you ought to think, but to think with sober judgment, each according to the measure of faith that God has assigned.
Romans 12:3

Reflection

Dear Child of God, the Lord wants us to consciously resist the inclination and temptation to be proud, to see ourselves as more important than others, the temptation to treat people with contempt and to exaggerate our own relevance. Yes, we are special before God but that should make us humble not proud, knowing full well that the glory in us comes from God and is not self-generated. Humility is the recognition of reality. Pride is not just an indication of spiritual immaturity but evidence of deluded thinking.

PRAYER

Lord Jesus, help me to see myself as you see me and to be humble as you have taught me.
Amen.

Day 12

BE HOLY AS I AM HOLY

⁷ Consecrate yourselves therefore and be
holy; for I am the Lord your God.
Leviticus 20:7

Reflection

The Lord wants us to consecrate ourselves and be holy, for He, our God is holy. To be holy means to set ourselves aside from anything that is sinful and displeasing to God. Since our God is all-holy, He demands holiness from all of us who worship Him. Dear Child of God, seek to separate yourself from any act, company, relationship, attraction and adventure that can offend the holiness of God.

PRAYER

Lord Jesus, help me to separate myself from anything that can stain my baptismal garment. May I seek and strive for holiness. Amen.

MARKED BY THE SEAL
OF THE SPIRIT

*13 In Him you also, when you had heard the
word of truth, the gospel of your salvation,
and had believed in Him, were marked with
the seal of the promised Holy Spirit.*
Ephesians 1:13

Reflection

Dear Child of God, keep in mind that you have
received the seal of the Holy Spirit on you. This is a
mark of ownership and security. This seal is also the
guarantee of our inheritance. Let us live as people
marked with a seal, people belonging to the Lord,
people hoping for an eternal inheritance. Do not allow
sin or carnal desires, carelessness and spiritual laziness
put a wrong stamp on your soul. Do not give the devil
the room to stamp his seal upon you.

PRAYER

Lord Jesus, thank you for the Holy Spirit which
is a seal upon me. May you O Lord, not take
away your Spirit from me as it was taken away
from Saul the king.
Amen.

Day 14

DO NOT BE A BURDEN TO ANYONE

[7] For you yourselves know how you ought to imitate us; we were not idle when we were with you, [8] and we did not eat anyone's bread without paying for it; but with toil and labour we worked night and day, so that we might not burden any of you.

2 Thessalonians 3:7-8

Reflection

Dear Child of God, as much as possible, try not to be a burden to anyone. Do whatever is within your power to help and support yourself. Sometimes we may not be able to deal with some things on our own but burdening others should not always be our first impulse. Sometimes people do not live according to their means. They choose a lifestyle, image or project they can't sustain without putting others under pressure and stress. Let us learn from St. Paul, who even while He laboured among the people of God, took care of himself by his work and he lived according to his means. A life of constant begging is not good enough for anyone.

PRAYER

Lord Jesus, teach me simplicity and humility. May I not project a false image or take delight in burdening others.
Amen.

GOD IS MY GOLD

25 and if the Almighty is your gold and your precious silver, 26 then you will delight yourself in the Almighty, and lift up your face to God.
Job 22:25-26

Reflection

Gold and Silver are very precious and desirable possessions. We all delight to have them, and we keep them carefully. They are great wealth. Using the analogy of gold and silver, Job tells us to also take delight in the Lord, to cherish our relationship with Him, to allow God to fill us with joy and happiness, to place our security in Him. No wealth is more than having God in our lives and when we have Him, we have all that we need because all that we need is in Him.

PRAYER

Lord Jesus, may I cherish my relationship with you more than I cherish the world's best gifts. Amen.

Day 16

GOD IS OUR REFUGE

*¹ God is our refuge and strength, a very
present help in trouble.
² Therefore we will not fear, though the
earth should change, though the mountains
shake in the heart of the sea;
³ though its waters roar and foam, though
the mountains tremble with its tumult.*
Psalm 46:1-3

Reflection

Dear Child of God, if we set our minds on things
happening around us, the situation of things in our
world, things going on around us and in our own lives,
we cannot but be afraid. However, we are reminded
today that God is our refuge, God is our stronghold. In
God is our confidence and so we can have peace amidst
the crises around us, knowing that our God is greater
than our problems.

PRAYER

Lord Jesus, in you I trust. I shall not fear; the
crises of life shall not overshadow me.
Amen.

Day 17

CHOSEN BEFORE THE WORLD WAS MADE

⁴ just as He chose us in Christ before the foundation of the world to be holy and blameless before Him in love.
Ephesians 1:4

Reflection

Dear Child of God, you are not an afterthought. You have been in the mind and plan of God from all eternity. You are not a mistake in the world but a significant part of a great plan. God chose you in Christ before the foundation of the world. He chose you not necessarily to be a world celebrity, a wealthy person, or a superstar, but to be holy. A holy person is God's celebrity. You are chosen to be God's celebrity.

PRAYER

Lord Jesus, you chose me to be holy. Help me to use all the means you have made available for me so that I may be holy and blameless before you.
Amen.

Day 18

THE TRUTH IN LOVE

25 So then, putting away falsehood, let all of us speak the truth to our neighbours, for we are members of one another.
Ephesians 4:25

Reflection

Dear Child of God, the Holy Spirit is the Spirit of truth. Jesus Himself is the truth and He has consecrated us in truth. Let us therefore put aside all falsehood, lies, deception, dishonesty and insincerity. We must make a decision relying on God's grace to always be truthful and say nothing which we know to be untrue.

PRAYER

Lord Jesus, you are the truth, and in you there is no deceit. Grant that I may be sincere and truthful always.
Amen.

REJOICE WITH THOSE WHO REJOICE

15 Rejoice with those who rejoice, weep with those who weep.
Romans 12:15

Reflection

Sometimes people love to weep with those who weep but are slow to rejoice with others. People are more eager to sympathise than to congratulate. As for you dear Child of God, do not rejoice when others are mourning, or share in people's pains. But do not be sad when something good happens to someone. Share in their joy and say no to the envy and hatred that often make us feel bad at seeing good things happen to others.

PRAYER

Lord Jesus, help me to support others in their mourning and rejoice with people as they rejoice in what you have done for them.
Amen.

Day 20

GOD DESERVES ALL YOUR ATTENTION

¹⁴ Do not follow other gods, any of the gods of the peoples who are all around you.
Deuteronomy 6:14

Reflection

Dear Child of God, God deserves all your love and your attention. No one and none else should be preferred or prioritised above God. Do not let anything compete with God in your life. Do not give to your family, job, relationship, association, party, career, or entertainment, the space in your heart that should be filled by God. Do not disobey God in order to obey any man or woman. Anyone who makes us disobey God is posing as an idol, a rival-god. Our God doesn't accommodate or co-exist with idols. He will never share His glory with anyone, and you are the glory of His works.

PRAYER

Lord Jesus, be the Lord and king in my life. I worship and lift you high above everything and everyone else.
Amen.

I WILL REMEMBER THEIR SINS NO MORE

[12] For I will be merciful toward their iniquities, and I will remember their sins no more.

Hebrews 8:12

Reflection

Often the devil wants to keep reminding us of what God wants us to forget and move on from. He wants to keep bringing back to our memories, sins of our earlier years. He wants us to feel guilty, worthless, unworthy, condemned and miserable. Dear Child of God, keep in mind today that whatever sins you have repented of, confessed and atoned for, the Lord no longer keeps account. Do not allow the devil to harass you anymore. The Lord says He will be merciful toward your iniquities and your sins He will remember no more.

PRAYER

Lord Jesus, thank you for your forgiveness and mercy. Help me to live in the peace that comes from the awareness that my sins and guilt have been washed away and I bear them no more. Amen.

Day 22

KEEP YOUR HEART WITH VIGILANCE

²³ Keep your heart with all vigilance, for from it flow the springs of life. ²⁴ Put away from you crooked speech and put devious talk far from you.
Proverbs 4:23-24

Reflection
Dear Child of God, the Lord wants us to preserve our heart, to keep it with all diligence. Let us be careful this day what we allow into our heart and those we open our hearts to. Remember that the state of our heart is very important to God and it is our duty to protect it against evil, impurity and deception.

PRAYER
Lord Jesus, I give you my heart. Let it beat for love of you. May I never allow my heart to be corrupted by anyone or anything.
Amen.

Day 23

HIS BANNER OVER ME IS LOVE

*⁴ He brought me to the banqueting house,
and His intention toward me was love.*
Songs 2:4

Reflection

Dear Child of God, God's feeling for you is pure love. His banner over you is love, the reason behind His goodness to you is love, the reason He chastises you is love, the reason He wants your heart is love. Do not ever think you are unloved, rejected or unwanted by God. God has chosen to love you unconditionally and it is constant and unchanging. What will be your response to this love?

PRAYER

Lord Jesus, thank you for loving me so much. May I show love in return for love. May I love with all my heart, He who loves and accepts me unconditionally.

Amen.

Day 24

DO NOT PAY BACK WITH EVIL

¹⁷ Do not repay anyone evil for evil but take thought for what is noble in the sight of all.
Romans 12:17

Reflection

Dear Child of God, has anyone hurt you, has anyone betrayed your trust, maligned you, harmed you, treated you unfairly or accused you wrongly? The flesh says "pay back with evil" but I say to you "listen to God's Spirit saying to you do not think any evil." Do not repay anyone with evil for evil, offer the hurt to the Lord. Let Him transform them to grace for you. This is how you turn your pains into gains.

PRAYER

Lord Jesus, I offer my hurt and pain to you. Remove from my heart any urge to repay evil. May nothing suffocate the fruit of love which the Holy Spirit has deposited in me.
Amen.

STAY AWAY FROM WRONG

¹Do no evil, and evil will never overtake you. ² Stay away from wrong, and it will turn away from you.
Sirach 7:1-2

Reflection

Dear Child of God, meditate on this as you face the challenges of today. Stay away from wrong, be intentional about doing what is right. People may think you are scrupulous, unclever and unadventurous but before God you are wise and prudent. Sometimes doing what is wrong seems a way to get to a desired goal or destination more quickly or a smarter way to achieve something but then it always ends in shame and regret. The end doesn't at any time justify the means.

PRAYER

Lord Jesus, help me to know what is right, to love what is right and insist on what is right and pleasing to you.
Amen.

Day 26

PURIFICATION FROM SPIRITUAL DEFILEMENT

*Since we have these promises, beloved, let us
cleanse ourselves from every defilement of
body and of spirit, making holiness perfect
in the fear of God.*
2 Corinthians 7:1

Reflection

Dear Child of God, St. Paul reminds us today that
since we have God's promise that He will be a Father
to us and we shall be His children, we ought to cleanse
ourselves from every defilement of body and spirit.
Note that defilement is not just something that
pertains to the flesh. Even our Spirit could be defiled.
Defilement of the spirit includes self-righteousness,
pride, self-focus, doubt, and fear. Let us try to
cooperate with the Spirit of God as He cleanses us daily
from all that seeks to defile our body and spirit.

PRAYER

Lord Jesus, I surrender to you to purify my Spirit
so that nothing in me impedes me from
worshipping you in truth.
Amen.

Day 27

SHOW KINDNESS

⁶ Mephibosheth son of Jonathan son of Saul came to David and fell on his face and did obeisance. David said, "Mephibosheth!" He answered, "I am your servant." ⁷ David said to him, "Do not be afraid, for I will show you kindness for the sake of your father Jonathan; I will restore to you all the land of your grandfather Saul, and you yourself shall eat at my table always."

2 Samuel 9:6-7

Reflection

David was kind to Mephibosheth, the son of Jonathan, because of the kindness shown to Him by Jonathan. He exalted and favoured Mephibosheth beyond his wildest imagination. Dear Child of God, the Lord also wants us to remember to show kindness to others, just as we have received. Let us never forget all those who have been kind to us. Let us show gratitude by being kind to them and others in return. Most particularly, let us remember God's kindness to us and show our gratitude by being kind to His children.

PRAYER

Lord Jesus, I am a testimony of your kindness. May others come to experience your kindness through me.

Amen.

Day 28

THE LORD'S IS THE EARTH

*¹ The earth is the Lord's and all that is in
it, the world, and those who live in it*
Psalm 24:1

Reflection

Dear Child of God, even though some people pose as if they are in control of events in the world, that they dictate the condition of human life and existence, the Lord wants you to keep in mind that the whole world belongs to Him, and everything and everyone therein. Everything belongs to Him by creation and continuous providence and sustenance. Hence, to Him be all worship, adoration and trust, for He owns the world and everything therein and from Him comes all that can make our lives meaningful.

PRAYER

Lord Jesus, help me to trust in you and to worship you as Lord of heaven and the whole earth.
Amen.

Day 29

KINDNESS TO STRANGERS

⁵ Beloved, you do faithfully whatever you do
for the friends, even though they are
strangers to you
3 John 1:5

Reflection

Dear Child of God, the Lord wants us to be very kind to everyone. He specially admonishes us to be kind to strangers. Being kind to strangers includes being willing to help them, make them feel comfortable, loved and accepted. There is a special blessing in being kind, hospitable and warm to strangers. This is a special calling for us as children of God.

PRAYER

Lord Jesus, teach me to be kind to everyone, especially to strangers. May I treat them with genuine love and be willing to help them.
Amen.

Day 30

THE DEBT OF LOVE

⁸Owe no one anything, except to love one another; for the one who loves another has fulfilled the law. ⁹ The commandments, "You shall not commit adultery; You shall not murder; You shall not steal; You shall not covet"; and any other commandment, are summed up in this word, "Love your neighbour as yourself."
Romans 13:8-9

Reflection

Dear Child of God, the summary of spirituality is charity. To love others is to fulfil the law. Let us keep in mind that love is a debt we owe to everyone, whether they deserve it or not. It is not a suggestion or a recommendation, it is a divine command, an obligation which is placed on us and which we must fulfil with joy. Let there be no shortage of love for anyone in your heart.

PRAYER

Lord Jesus, help me to love others as I love myself or better still as you love me, for your love for me is better than my love for myself. Amen.

THEY CRIED TO THE LORD

⁶ Thus Israel was greatly impoverished because of Midian; and the Israelites cried out to the Lord for help. ⁷ When the Israelites cried to the Lord on account of the Midianites.
Judges 6:6

Reflection

The Israelites suffered so much under the Midianites; their crops were destroyed, their lives were made miserable, their joy was taken away. In their sorrow, they faced heaven and God heard their cry. Dear Child of God, do you feel under the oppression, manipulation or threat of anyone? Are you having to endure a humiliating condition and can see no way out? The Lord who delivered the Israelites is able to deliver you from all the Midianites in your life. You cannot live the life of a victim when you have a God who is Almighty.

PRAYER

Lord Jesus, deliver me from those who bear hatred against me, those who watch for my downfall.
Amen.

SEPTEMBER

Day 1

LIVING ON PAST GLORY

24 But when the righteous turn away from their righteousness and commit iniquity and do the same abominable things that the wicked do, shall they live? None of the righteous deeds that they have done shall be remembered; for the treachery of which they are guilty and the sin they have committed, they shall die.
Ezekiel 18:24

Reflection

Often people say I used to be this, I used to be that in the Church, I was a good Christian, I was once... Dear Child of God, God doesn't judge us according to who or what we were but according to who we are now. Let your sins be in the past but not your righteousness because the past is the past and who you are before God now is what matters.

PRAYER

Lord Jesus, help me to live today for you and not rely on the past for vindication.
Amen.

Day 2

TEST EVERYTHING

*²¹ ....but test everything; hold fast to
what is good.*
1 Thessalonians 5:21

Reflection

There is so much deceit in our world today, so much
false doctrine, opinion, perverted gospel, misleading
information, and superstition in the garment of faith.
As for you dear Child of God, the Lord wants you to
have a soft heart that is loving and merciful but not a
soft head that believes even error. Pray therefore for
discernment.

PRAYER

Lord Jesus, give me the Spirit of discernment so
that I may differentiate between what is from
you and what is not.
Amen.

TREASURE IN CLAY JARS

⁷ But we have this treasure in clay jars, so that it may be made clear that this extraordinary power belongs to God and does not come from us.
2 Corinthians 4:7

Reflection

Dear Child of God, God has deposited so much in us. We are a huge divine investment. He has given us so many gifts, graces, charisms and talents. He has deposited so much power in us. Let us keep in mind that all these are from God and we are clay jars holding divine treasures. Let us be careful of pride and let us be careful how we live, so that the clay jar doesn't lose that which is in it.

PRAYER

Lord Jesus, protect all that you have deposited in me. May I always remember that whatever is good in me comes from you.
Amen.

Day 4

CREATED IN HIS IMAGE

*²⁷ So God created humankind in His image,
in the image of God He created them; male
and female He created them.*
Genesis 1:27

Reflection

Dear Child of God, every human person you see is divine. Yes, because he/she is a bearer of the divine image. Among all God's creature, the human person is the greatest because God created us in His own image. He endowed us with a spirit that can yearn for Him, with memory to remember His goodness to us in the past, with a will to choose what is right and wrong and an immortal soul that will reunite with Him for all eternity. With this in mind, let us treat every human person irrespective of age, race, gender, status or condition with respect, love and dignity.

PRAYER

Lord Jesus, thank you for your image in me. Help me to respect you in me and you in others too.
Amen.

CREATED FOR GOOD WORKS

¹⁰ For we are what He has made us, created in Christ Jesus for good works, which God prepared beforehand to be our way of life.
Ephesians 2:10

Reflection

Some philosophers say existence precedes essence. In other words, we exist and try to find our purpose in life by ourselves. Dear Child of God, you are not created to look for your purpose, God has a purpose for creating you. He has an assignment for you, and He brought you into existence at the right season for the right reason. Let us be close to God and ask Him daily to lead us to fulfil the essence of our existence before we return to Him.

PRAYER

Lord Jesus, show me my essence in life, my space in the overall scheme of things and strengthen me to fulfil my purpose for your glory.
Amen.

Day 6

YOU ARE SPECIAL BECAUSE HE CHOSE YOU

⁷ It was not because you were more numerous than any other people that the Lord set His heart on you and chose you— for you were the fewest of all peoples.
Deuteronomy 7:7

Reflection

Dear Child of God, you are not chosen by God because you are special, you are special because God chose you. He chose you as His. We have not done anything special to deserve what we have received from God but having received from God and having been chosen by God we must work harder to show our gratitude to God for counting us worthy among those whom He has called and chosen to be His own.

PRAYER

Lord Jesus, thank you for choosing me to be your beloved child. May I live each day in the awareness of the privilege of belonging to you. Amen.

SELF-ENEMIES

⁹ For almsgiving saves from death and purges away every sin. Those who give alms will enjoy a full life, ¹⁰ but those who commit sin and do wrong are their own worst enemies.

Tobit 12:9-10

Reflection

Dear Child of God, do not be an enemy unto yourself. Anyone who rejects God's love and continues in sin is an enemy of him/herself. Anyone who is unkind to others is an enemy of his/her self. Anyone who refuses to repent from sin, even with the knowledge that sin leads to eternal damnation, such a person is an enemy of him/herself. The person who fights an innocent person or someone favoured by God, such is an enemy of him/herself. Do not be an enemy of yourself; be grateful to God for who you are and avoid anything that can lead you to regret.

PRAYER

Lord Jesus, help me to soak myself in your love and to avoid turning against myself.
Amen.

Day 8

DO NOT FORGET YOUR TRUE FRIENDS

¹⁰ Do not abandon old friends, for new ones cannot equal them. A new friend is like new wine; when it has aged, you can drink it with pleasure.
Sirach 9:10

Reflection

When we meet new friends, there is a delight and pleasure that we have. However, we should not forget all those who have been there for us, the shoulders we once cried on, our old friends who really shaped us and supported us in our earlier days. No matter how blessed and privileged we may be, let us remember those who made a difference in our lives and support as many of them as we may be able to support. Dear Child of God, let us always be good friends to others and not allow time, pride, petty quarrels to come between us and those whom God has placed in our lives for all seasons.

PRAYER

Lord Jesus, thank you for my friends both old and new. Help me to support all those who call me their friend and to cherish all those who are faithful friends to me.
Amen.

HE IS MERCIFUL AND JUST

⁵ Now I desire to remind you, though you are fully informed, that the Lord, who once for all saved a people out of the land of Egypt, afterward destroyed those who did not believe.

Jude 1:5

Reflection

Often people say God is so merciful, He will pardon all offences, He won't punish anyone nor allow anyone to go to hell. St. Jude reminds us today that we should think of God's mercy along with His justice. It was He who saved His people from bondage out of His mercy and in justice, He punished those who refused to believe in Him. Dear Child of God, do not take the mercy of God for granted and do not provoke His wrath.

PRAYER

Lord Jesus, thank you for your mercy in my life. May I never take your mercy for granted. Amen.

Day 10

HE GIVES GRACE TO THE HUMBLE

⁶But He gives all the more grace; therefore it says, "God opposes the proud, but gives grace to the humble."
James 4:6

Reflection

Dear Child of God, when we look at Jesus we see great humility. Though His nature was divine, He humbled Himself and became like us. He shared our lowly human condition, He accepted birth in a manger, He was available and accessible to all, He mixed with the lowly, poor, sinners, outcast, those at the margin of society. He even calls us His friends. Let us learn from Jesus to be truly humble and to not treat anyone with contempt or disrespect. Let us not be haughty but be meek like Christ. Humility exalts a person, but pride resists the flow of grace in us.

PRAYER

Lord Jesus, make me truly humble as you are, for in humility and showing mercy I resemble you very closely.
Amen.

ABUNDANCE OF LIFE IS IN JESUS ALONE

[10] The thief comes only to steal and kill and destroy. I came that they may have life and have it abundantly.
John 10:10

Reflection

Dear Child of God, the agenda of the devil is to make you miserable and spiritually poor. He wants to steal your heavenly inheritance, to kill you spiritually by separating you from the source of life and to destroy your joy, your peace, your faith, your happiness, your family, vocation, future, your self-esteem and your life. Do not allow him - stand up to him, resist him and embrace the life that Jesus wants for you. This is a life of joy and peace, a good life in this world and a blessed eternity in the world to come.

PRAYER

Lord Jesus, I thank you for the gift of abundant life in you. May I live the life you want for me and not what the enemy plans for me.
Amen.

Day 12
THE SUPPLEMENTS TO FAITH

*⁵ For this very reason, you must make every effort
to support your faith with goodness, and goodness
with knowledge, ⁶ and knowledge with self-
control, and self-control with endurance, and
endurance with godliness.*

2 Peter 1:5-6

Reflection

Dear Child of God, it is not enough to say that I have
faith, that I believe in God. Faith must be shown in
good actions. Good actions must be supplemented
with knowledge. We must know what we believe and
why we do what we do. To knowledge we must add
self-control because faith, goodness and knowledge
without self-control will lead to pride and arrogance.
We must also endure in our faith and goodness, in
what we know and in putting our self under check. All
of this must be guided by the love of God and the
desire to please God, not ourselves - this is godliness.
Faith doesn't stand alone; it is a bundle. If any of
goodness, knowledge, self-control, endurance and
godliness is missing, then the bundle is not complete.

PRAYER

Lord Jesus bless me with living and firm faith
that works through loving action.
Amen.

CAPTIVES FROM THE MIGHTY

²⁴ Can the prey be taken from the mighty, or the captives of a tyrant be rescued? ²⁵ But thus says the Lord: Even the captives of the mighty shall be taken, and the prey of the tyrant be rescued; for I will contend with those who contend with you, and I will save your children.

Isaiah 49:24-25

Reflection

Dear Child of God, our God is a deliverer. The one who delivered Daniel from the den of lions is still in the business of delivering His own. Let us call on Him always to deliver us from the snares of the devil and his agent, to deliver us from enemies who appear to us as friends, to deliver us from those who shoot at us from the dark, from evil men and woman, from all workers of iniquities, to deliver us from every power and force working against us and trying to hold us captive.

PRAYER

Lord Jesus, you are able and willing to deliver those who trust in you. Do not allow me to be held captive by evil forces and people but be my salvation.
Amen.

Day 14

A CARRIER OF BLESSING

²⁷ But Laban said to him, "If you will allow me to say so, I have learned by divination that the Lord has blessed me because of you.
Genesis 30:27

Reflection

The presence of Jacob in the house of Laban brought Laban great blessing. While some people are bearers of blessings, some are just negative people with negative vibes. We need to be careful who we let into our hearts and those we allow into our families. As for you dear Child of God, God's goodness and mercy are following you everywhere you go.

PRAYER

Lord Jesus, make me a source of blessing just like Jacob, so that everywhere I go, I may be a bearer of your blessing.
Amen.

Day 15
THE CROWN OF LIFE

[12] Blessed is anyone who endures temptation. Such a one has stood the test and will receive the crown of life that the Lord has promised to those who love Him.
James 1:12

Reflection

Dear Child of God, Jesus has prepared for you a crown of life, a crown of glory, but before we take possession, we must go through temptations, we must demonstrate that our love for God is above our love for all other things in life. The crown of life shall only be won by those who have proven that they love God more than anything else in this world.

PRAYER

Lord Jesus, may your love increase in me daily until I love you above all that the world has to offer. May I never fall into temptation but be made strong against these temptations.
Amen.

Day 16

HE FORGIVES IF WE CONFESS

*⁸ If we say that we have no sin, we deceive
ourselves, and the truth is not in us. ⁹ If we confess
our sins, He who is faithful and just will forgive us
our sins and cleanse us from all unrighteousness.*
1 John 1:8-9

Reflection

Dear Child of God, God is very loving and forgiving.
He is even more patient and forgiving to us than we
are to one another. However, to obtain His
forgiveness, we must acknowledge that we are sinners.
We must not pretend to be righteous or conceal our
sins. Even when we confess to Him we are not telling
Him what He doesn't know, we are only
acknowledging that we are aware of our sins and that
we stand in need of His forgiveness. If we are truly
sorry and we come to Him with sincere contrition
without self-justification or shifting blame to others,
He forgives us completely.

PRAYER

Lord Jesus, have mercy on me a poor sinner.
Give me strength to overcome my weaknesses
and my inclination to sin.
Amen.

KEEP YOURSELF IN GOD'S LOVE

²¹ ... keep yourselves in the love of God; look forward to the mercy of our Lord Jesus Christ that leads to eternal life.
Jude 1:21

Reflection

Dear Child of God, the love of God is open to all, but we must keep ourselves where it can reach us. The sun shines and gives warmth but we must keep ourselves within its reach. The prodigal son kept himself from where the love of his father could reach him. He wasn't experiencing love in a faraway land, not because the father stopped loving him but because he had shut himself out of that love.

Let us not place ourselves where the love of God won't touch us but keep ourselves close to Him and within His ray of love.

PRAYER

Lord Jesus, let me always remain in the ray of your love. Never let me stray away from your light and love.
Amen.

Day 18

HE DOESN'T CLEAR THE GUILTY

³ The Lord is slow to anger but great in power, and the Lord will by no means clear the guilty. His way is in whirlwind and storm, and the clouds are the dust of His feet.
Nahum 1:3

Reflection

The Lord is very merciful, but His mercy doesn't mean He clears the guilty whether in time or eternity. Every sin we commit must be paid for. It could either be paid for on the cross or in hell. Those who accept the sacrifice of Jesus and repent of their sins and make atonement shall experience the mercy of God. Those who obstinately persist in their sins and guilt, no matter how nicely people speak about them, will pay for their misdeeds in hell.

PRAYER

Lord Jesus, help me repent of my sins and let me experience your great mercy.
Amen.

Day 19

FAITH COMES THROUGH HEARING

*So faith comes from what is heard, and
what is heard comes through the Word of
Christ.*
Romans 10:17

Reflection

Dear Child of God, faith comes from hearing or reading the Word of God and accepting what it contains. The more we feed our heart with the Word of God, the more we increase in faith. Let us therefore be committed to seek every opportunity to listen to God's Word, to study and ponder on it and ask the Lord for a deeper understanding. Let us also seek to help others to hear the Word of God so that faith may also grow in them.

PRAYER

Lord Jesus, create in me a new spirit that hungers for your Word and as I feed on it, increase my faith and use it to ignite faith in others.
Amen.

Day 20

NOT A SPIRIT OF COWARDICE

*..... for God did not give us a spirit of
cowardice, but rather a spirit of power and
of love and of self-discipline.*
2 Timothy 1:7

Reflection

Dear Child of God, the Holy Spirit is not the spirit of
cowardice. The spirit of cowardice is that which recoils
from fulfilling God's mandate out of fear. It is the spirit
that mutes us so as to avoid judgements, criticism and
questions. It is the spirit that denies Christ and is
ashamed to proclaim one's faith. It is the spirit that
cannot say no to evil and challenge injustice. Dear
Child of God, you have received from God, the spirit
of power to witness to Christ and what is true, right
and just. You have received love to be able to witness
in charity and self-control, to restrain the impulse to
outstep our bounds or act outside of sensible
proportion.

PRAYER

Lord Jesus, take away from me the spirit of
cowardice and fill me with your power, love and
self-control.
Amen.

Day 21

THE HOLY SPIRIT WILL TEACH YOU

But the Advocate, the Holy Spirit, whom the Father will send in my name, will teach you everything, and remind you of all that I have said to you.
John 14:26

Reflection

Dear Child of God, one of the greatest gifts that we have received from God through Christ is the Holy Spirit. The Holy Spirit is to be our comforter, our counsellor, our advocate. The Holy Spirit convicts us of sins. He is a teacher and He reminds us of what Christ has taught us. Let us consciously seek to grow in intimacy with the Holy Spirit to make our relationship with God better and our Spiritual life more alive and active.

PRAYER

Lord Jesus, I open myself to the Holy Spirit. May I receive His help and through Him grow spiritually unto maturity.
Amen.

Day 22

RESCUED FROM THE POWER OF DARKNESS

¹³ He has rescued us from the power of darkness and transferred us into the kingdom of His beloved Son, ¹⁴ in whom we have redemption, the forgiveness of sins.
Colossians 1:13-14

Reflection

The Lord has rescued all those who believe and accept Him from the power of darkness. We are now transferred into God's kingdom of light. We are beneficiaries of Christ's redemption and our sins have been forgiven. Dear Child of God, we are no longer under the power of the devil. We are not his slaves, he is not our king. We do not obey him, and we must not bow to his temptation. We are people who are redeemed and our sins and guilt, which are barriers between us and God, have been taken away. Let us be careful not to willingly surrender ourselves to darkness after being rescued by Christ. Let us ensure that nothing of the devil remains with us.

PRAYER

Lord Jesus, thank you for delivering me from the kingdom of darkness. Help me to live always as a subject of your kingdom of light.
Amen.

Day 23

THE FRUIT OF THE SPIRIT

*²² By contrast, the fruit of the Spirit is love,
joy, peace, patience, kindness, generosity,
faithfulness, ²³ gentleness, and self-control.
There is no law against such things.*
Galatians 5:22

Reflection

Dear Child of God, examine your life. The power controlling your life will reflect in the fruit you bear. If you live according to the Spirit, it will show in a life of love, joy, peace, patience, kindness, generosity, faithfulness, gentleness and self-control. What a beautiful way to live. These are the good fruits that make the Christian life pleasant and attractive to others.

PRAYER

Lord Jesus, may I be rooted in the Holy Spirit and bear good and rich fruits.
Amen.

Day 24

IN THE ABSENCE OF LOVE

*If I speak in the tongues of mortals and of
angels, but do not have love, I am a noisy
gong or a clanging cymbal. And if I have
prophetic powers, and understand all
mysteries and all knowledge, and if I have
all faith, so as to remove mountains, but do
not have love, I am nothing. If I give away
all my possessions, and if I hand over my
body so that I may boast, but do not have
love, I gain nothing.*
1 Corinthians 1:1-3

Reflection

Without love, our gifts and charism, sacrifice and piety,
worship and devotion will be bereft of value. It is
through sincere love that we can testify to the world
that we know the Lord. If a man has faith that can move
mountains and has no love, he will move the mountain
into someone else's way or onto someone's head. What
God requires of all of us principally is to love. Love is
the greatest gift, fruit and grace.

PRAYER

Lord Jesus, give me a heart of true love like
yours.
Amen.

FEAR OF THE LORD

*Is not your fear of God your confidence, and
the integrity of your ways your hope?*
Job 4:6

Reflection

To fear the Lord is to be careful to avoid whatever
offends Him, not because we do not want to be
punished but because we do not want to disappoint
someone who has loved us so much. When we live in
fear of God, we live in confidence and when we seek
to walk in integrity, we walk securely. Even when we
are falsely accused or taunted, fear of the Lord and
integrity will always vindicate us.

PRAYER

Lord Jesus, help me to avoid whatever offends
the Lord. May I diligently walk in integrity and
the fear of the Lord.
Amen.

Day 26

OBEDIENCE TO GOD FIRST

*But the midwives feared God; they did not
do as the king of Egypt commanded them,
but they let the boys live.*
Exodus 1:17

Reflection

The midwives of Egypt were commanded by Pharaoh to do what was evil. However, they obeyed their conscience and avoided the evil. Though Pharaoh was very powerful, and their lives were at stake, out of mercy and fear of God, they would rather stake their lives than shed innocent blood against their conscience. Dear Child of God, keep in mind, that obedience to authorities or anyone is never an obligation when it means disobeying God and violating our conscience. Our loyalty must first be to the King of kings before any earthly king.

PRAYER

Lord Jesus, help me to keep in mind always that obedience to you supersedes obedience to any human person.
Amen.

Day 27

THE SPIRIT WILL CONVICT AND REVEAL

⁸And when He comes, He will prove the world wrong about sin and righteousness and judgment
John 16:8

Reflection

There are many wrong things we do today, but we excuse ourselves and we justify them. People have devised euphemisms for sins and call them by good names. Often we have pushed freedom beyond the bounds of reason. We have come to accept as normal what is abominable before God. Jesus reminds us today that we need the Holy Spirit to help us see sins for what they are. More than ever before, we need the help of the Holy Spirit to rid us of our self-deception, tolerance of sin, erroneous opinions and false beliefs.

PRAYER

Lord Jesus, I pray that the Holy Spirit may enlighten me and free me from false beliefs and erroneous opinion about sin, righteousness and judgement.
Amen.

Day 28

FAITH IN TRIALS

²My brothers and sisters, whenever you face trials of any kind, consider it nothing but joy, ³ because you know that the testing of your faith produces endurance; ⁴ and let endurance have its full effect, so that you may be mature and complete, lacking in nothing.
James 1:2-4

Reflection

St. James teaches us how to respond to our trials of life. Dear Child of God, we are to receive our trials with faith. When we do this, it produces patience and we become more mature through what we go through in life. However, if difficulties are received without trusting in God, trials can produce bitterness and discouragement.

PRAYER

Lord Jesus, give me the grace to accept my trials with courage and faith.
Amen.

Day 29

SEEK THE LORD AND LIVE

*⁶ Seek the Lord and live, or He will
break out against the house of Joseph
like fire, and it will devour Bethel,
with no one to quench it.*
Amos 5:6

Reflection

Israel was ripe for judgement; the key to survival was simply to seek the Lord. To seek the Lord means to turn to Him, to repent of our sins and confess our need of Him. When we turn to the Lord, we allow His mercy to envelop us. Dear Child of God, there is hope of mercy, forgiveness and pardon for you if you will seek the Lord earnestly.

PRAYER

Lord Jesus, let me always seek you and through seeking you, feel your mercy and love.
Amen.

Day 30

HONOUR YOUR PARENTS

*⁸ Hear, my child, your father's instruction,
and do not reject your mother's teaching;
⁹ for they are a fair garland for your head,
and pendants for your neck.*
Proverbs 1:8-9

Reflection

No matter how wise, rich, intelligent and independent we may feel we are, the Lord does not want us to despise our parents for any reason. We must always keep in mind that when we honour our parents, we honour God and we prepare a good future for ourselves. Dear Child of God, if your parents are still alive, please do all you can to make them feel loved. If you need to forgive or reconcile, please do. If they have departed this world, remember them in your prayers.

PRAYER

Lord Jesus, bless our parents and help us to honour them through prayers, through obedience to them, adequate care and generous love. Amen.

OCTOBER

Day 1

CALLED TO TESTIFY

*³⁴ And I myself have seen and have testified
that this is the Son of God.*
John 1:34

Reflection

John testified and told people about Jesus. Note what
he said: *And I myself have seen and have testified...* We are
all called to testify to Jesus, but we must first see, we
must first encounter Him. We can only testify
adequately, accurately and convincingly about what we
have encountered, experienced and are familiar with.
Let us therefore pray today that we may know the Lord
more and be able to testify that He is Lord and saviour.

PRAYER

Lord Jesus, I want to know you more and be
able to testify that you are the Lord.
Amen.

Day 2

OUR FAITH IS THE CANON

²³ But those who have doubts are
condemned if they eat, because they do not
act from faith; for whatever does not
proceed from faith is sin.
Romans 14:23

Reflection

Here, St. Paul gives us a principle by which we can judge all our actions. Whatever we love but doesn't agree with faith or can hinder our closer walk with God, is sinful. This means before we approve of anything, we ought to ask, is it in accordance with my faith? What will this contribute to my spiritual life and my relationship with God? Dear Child of God, let your faith be a factor in judging whatever you approve or disapprove in your life.

PRAYER

Lord Jesus, in whatever I do, may I put my faith first in consideration and avoid anything that can jeopardise it.
Amen.

Day 3

VESSELS FOR SPECIAL USE

*20 In a large house there are utensils not
only of gold and silver but also of wood and
clay, some for special use, some for ordinary.*
2 Timothy 2:20

Reflection

Dear Child of God, what type of vessel are you? St.
Paul says there are different vessels in a large house;
some are for special use and some for ordinary. When
we surrender our will to the Lord like Mary did and we
do not give sin the permission to disfigure our lives, we
shall be a treasured vessel for special use in the hand of
God.

PRAYER

Lord Jesus, make me a vessel for special use, to
give you glory and praise as long as I live.
Amen.

TO DESTROY THE WORK OF THE DEVIL

8 Everyone who commits sin is a child of the devil; for the devil has been sinning from the beginning. The Son of God was revealed for this purpose, to destroy the works of the devil.

1 John 3:8

Reflection

Dear Child of God, Jesus has come to destroy the work of the devil in our lives. He has come to set us free from bondage of sin, to restore what the devil has stolen, to ransom us from his kingdom, to reveal and foil his schemes, to rescue us from his whims and caprices, to strengthen us against his temptations, to deliver us from fear of the devil. Let us therefore praise God for the revelation of the Son of Man. Let us come under His authority that He might reveal and defeat the plans of the devil against us.

PRAYER

Lord Jesus, I come under your authority. May the evil one not have the final say in my life. Amen.

Day 5

THE LORD WANTS ALL TO BE SAVED

³⁰ What then are we to say? Gentiles, who did not strive for righteousness, have attained it, that is, righteousness through faith.
Romans 9:30

Reflection

Dear Child of God, God has made provision for all of us to be saved. He doesn't limit salvation and His blessings to a particular group. St. Paul rejoices today in the salvation of the Gentiles and their attainment of righteousness through faith. As we rejoice in our own salvation, let us pray diligently that others may come to experience salvation in Christ Jesus. Let us pray most particularly for the conversion of hardened sinners, that the grace of God may restore them to righteousness through faith.

PRAYER

Lord Jesus, thank you for opening the door of salvation to everyone through faith. May those who have rejected your love, hear your call again and come back to salvation.
Amen.

FAITH NOT BASED ON SIGNS

48 Then Jesus said to him, "Unless you see signs and wonders you will not believe."
John 4:48

Reflection

Dear Child of God, a faith that is built on a solid foundation doesn't look for signs and wonders. Many are those who witness signs and wonders and yet their lives remain untransformed. Let us pray that the Lord will give us the gift of faith, to believe what He has said in His word, to hold firm to what He has promised us, to accept what the Church teaches and to be established and rooted in this faith.

PRAYER

Lord Jesus, I believe in all you have said and all that the Holy Spirit continues to say through the Church. May I not base my faith on signs and wonders, but on the authority of a God who doesn't lie or change.
Amen.

Day 7

I WILL TEACH YOU WHAT TO SPEAK

*¹² Now go, and I will be with your mouth
and teach you what you are to speak.*
Exodus 4:12

Reflection

Dear Child of God, our words are very important.
Words are measures of character and wisdom. Words
can save us from trouble or cause trouble. Words can
earn blessing or attract a curse. Let us be careful what
we say today, the jokes we crack, the content of our
speech and what escapes from our mouth. Let us
always beg the Lord to sanctify our words so that they
become right, acceptable, seasoned with grace and very
appropriate.

PRAYER

Lord Jesus, be glorified today in my words as
well as my silence. May nothing escape from my
mouth that won't gain your approval.
Amen.

291

YOU WON'T SEEK ME IN VAIN

*¹⁹ I did not speak in secret, in a land of
darkness; I did not say to the offspring of
Jacob, "Seek me in vain." I the Lord speak
the truth, I declare what is right.*
Isaiah 45:19

Reflection

Dear Child of God, God says when we seek Him, we
will find Him. He has not left you to seek Him in vain.
He does hide His face from you when you seek Him.
Whatever He commands is just, whatever He permits
is for a purpose, whatever He declares is right and
whatever the Lord speaks is true.

Let us then seek the Lord with all our heart and we
shall find Him and rest in His love.

PRAYER

Lord Jesus, I seek your face this day. Hide not
your face from me.
Amen.

Day 9
FAITH IS CONVICTION

*'Now faith is the assurance of things hoped
for, the conviction of things not seen.*
Hebrews 11:1

Reflection
Physical eyesight produces a conviction or evidence of
visible things. Faith is that which enables people to see
the invisible order. Faith gives us evidence of the
invisible, spiritual world. Faith goes beyond reason but
doesn't contradict it. It is not just an intellectual
understanding or mere belief that something is true,
faith is a willingness to rely, trust, cling to and lean on
God. Faith gives meaning to our human life and
existence. Let us pray for deeper faith in God and faith
greater than our crises of life.

PRAYER
Lord Jesus, increase my faith in you. Help me to
cling to you as my only hope.
Amen.

YOU WILL SEE THE GLORY OF GOD

⁴⁰ Jesus said to her, "Did I not tell you that if you believed, you would see the glory of God?"
John 11:40

Reflection

Dear Child of God, if we believe what God has promised, taught and revealed, if we believe that to God nothing is impossible and our situation is not beyond God, if we believe that God is not an idea or force or illusion but our loving Father who cares for us and who holds the whole world in His hands, we shall see the glory and power of God working through our lives and our situation.

PRAYER

Lord Jesus, I believe in you. May your glory shine upon my life.
Amen.

Day 11

THE CONQUERORS

⁷⁷ But they have conquered him by the blood of the Lamb and by the word of their testimony, for they did not cling to life even in the face of death.
Revelation 12:11

Reflection

Life is a battle conquered for us by Christ and so He has established an inheritance for us but to attain it, we must win in the battle of life. We win by the blood of Jesus and by confessing His lordship in our lives. We win when we love God more than our lives and when for His sake, we do not hold too tightly unto life. Conquerors cherish life but they cherish eternal life more and when they have to choose, they choose eternal life over life; they choose to die than to disobey God.

PRAYER

Lord Jesus, as much as I love life, may I not seek to preserve it at the detriment of eternal life with you.
Amen.

Day 12

LOYALTY WILL BE TESTED

[32] He shall seduce with intrigue those who violate the covenant; but the people who are loyal to their God shall stand firm and take action.

Daniel 11:32

Reflection

Dear Child of God, let us be firm and constant in our commitment and loyalty to God. Our loyalty shall always be tested, our allegiance and promise to God will be shaken. Let us be prepared, let us pray that God will supply grace to complement our resolve to be steadfast and not disappoint Him through compromise.

PRAYER

Lord Jesus, I declare my loyalty to you. May nothing shake or tempt me to compromise. Amen.

Day 13

ATHEISM IS FOOLISHNESS

[1] Fools say in their hearts, "There is no God." They are corrupt, they do abominable deeds; there is no one who does good.
Psalm 14:1

Reflection

It is foolishness to think there is no God. The evidence of God is everywhere, most particularly in us. Yes, every human person is a carrier of His breath, His image and likeness. Now and again, we see His intervention in our lives and history. However, foolishness is not just in declaring that there is no God, greater foolishness is in living as if God doesn't matter, and living corrupt, wicked and irresponsible lives. Dear Child of God, whether we believe or not, we shall all render account of our lives to the God who brought us into existence.

PRAYER

Lord Jesus, save me from foolishness and from a foolish way of thinking and living.
Amen.

Day 14

THE ARMOUR OF SPIRITUAL WARFARE

[14] Stand therefore, and fasten the belt of truth around your waist, and put on the breastplate of righteousness. [15] As shoes for your feet put on whatever will make you ready to proclaim the gospel of peace.
Ephesians 6:14-15

Reflection

Dear Child of God, we are reminded to be fully armed spiritually at all times. Let us fasten the belt of truth; that is, we must know and hold on to the truth, not error, heresy or false teaching. We must put on the breastplate of righteousness; that is, we must be right with God. We must rely on the righteousness of Christ and seek to be upright before God too. We must be ready to proclaim the Gospel of peace, because it is the power of God for the salvation of mankind. Let us not be complacent. Let us not give the devil a chance. Let us be always ready, fully armed with truth, righteousness and the message of the Gospel.

PRAYER

Lord Jesus, preserve me in truth and righteousness and let my mouth also proclaim your Gospel of peace.
Amen.

Day 15

UNLESS WE RELY TOTALLY ON GOD

¹² Therefore the Israelites are unable to stand before their enemies; they turn their backs to their enemies, because they have become a thing devoted for destruction themselves. I will be with you no more, unless you destroy the devoted things from among you.

Joshua 7:12

Reflection

God promised to defend His people, but they must first rely totally on Him for help. The Israelites kept in their custody what the Lord forbade. They violated what God had commanded and so they were defeated in battle by their enemies. Dear Child of God, disobedience to God costs us more than we can imagine. Let us keep in mind that in God is our hope and trust and as this is so, we must stop trying to do things in our own way and on our own terms. It is not enough to say the Lord is with us, we must also at every time be with the Lord.

PRAYER

Lord Jesus, save me from anything that may push me out of God's protection and favour. May I not hold unto anything that gives false security, nor turn my eyes from the Lord. Amen.

THE PEACEMAKERS

*⁹ Blessed are the peacemakers, for they will
be called children of God.*
Matthew 5:9

Reflection

Dear Child of God, remember it's part of your mission
to be an agent of peace. It is not enough to pray for
peace, we must also work for peace, speak words of
peace, help to reconcile people's differences and settle
those at loggerheads. We ought to avoid word and
action or sentiment that can destroy peace. You are a
peace maker and not a cause of division and trouble.
When we stand and work for peace, we are blessed by
God, honoured in the sight of others and we witness
that we are children of God.

PRAYER

Lord Jesus, make me an instrument of your
peace; where there is hatred, disunity and
conflict, may you sow love through me.
Amen.

Day 17

FIGHT THE GOOD FIGHT

*¹² Fight the good fight of the faith; take hold
of the eternal life, to which you were called
and for which you made the good confession
in the presence of many witnesses.*

1 Timothy 6:12

Reflection

Dear Child of God, you are reminded to be a fighter;
yes, we are called to be fighters. We are not weak and
helpless victims. We are fighters but let us not fight
senselessly. Let us not fight innocent people, let us not
fight the wrong battles. Let us fight the fight of faith.
This is fighting to claim our salvation. The kingdom of
God suffers violence and only the violent are taking it
by force. Let us have the determination of a soldier.
Going God's way against the flow of this world won't
be easy. Saying no to the flesh won't be easy. Resisting
the temptations of the devil won't be easy. Standing
against enemies of our salvation won't be easy but then
the Lord of hosts is with us. We are on the winning
side.

PRAYER

Lord Jesus, give me the strength and the power
of the Spirit to fight the good faith until I lay
hold of what you have promised me.
Amen.

Day 18

NO ONE CAN HARM YOUR SOUL

*¹³ Now who will harm you if you are eager
to do what is good?*
1 Peter 3:13

Reflection

We live in a strange but real world where our goodness is sometimes repaid with evil, where we suffer for doing what is right and are hated for not compromising our values. But the Word of the Lord tells us, "who will harm us if we do good?" This means that even though people can harm our body, they have no access to our soul. The harm of the body is merely temporal. The greatest harm is the harm done to the soul. Dear Child of God, our soul can never be harmed when we do good. Though we may suffer in the flesh for being upright, our soul rejoices because to suffer in the body for doing good will become a great profit for our soul.

PRAYER

Lord Jesus, may I not fear those who can harm my body but can't touch my soul. Rather, may I fear He who can chastise me both body and soul.
Amen.

Day 19

GOD DWELLS WITH THE HUMBLE AND CONTRITE

¹⁵ For thus says the high and lofty one who inhabits eternity, whose name is Holy: I dwell in the high and holy place, and also with those who are contrite and humble in spirit, to revive the spirit of the humble, and to revive the heart of the contrite.
Isaiah 57:15

Reflection

Dear Child of God, God has given us His address, where He can be found, where He dwells. He dwells in the highest heaven, He dwells in His holy temple. He also dwells in those who are contrite and humble in spirit. When we express sorrow for sins and humble ourselves before God, God works in us. He revives us and renews His Spirit in us.

PRAYER

Lord Jesus, I open the door of my heart to you. Come and dwell and remain with me and in me forever.
Amen.

THE COUNSEL OF THE LORD STANDS FIRM

*¹¹ The counsel of the Lord stands forever,
the thoughts of His heart to all generations.*
Psalm 33:11

Reflection

What the Lord wills no one can change. What the Lord has decreed, no one can revoke. We may say things and it will be altered by someone superior to us, but what the Lord has decided no one can revise. What He has said about you, no one can alter. What He has in mind for you, no one can change. Do not feel threatened or disturbed by whatever anyone is saying against you. Hold unto what the Lord says about you. In the long run, it is His counsel that matters.

PRAYER

Lord Jesus, your word is final and your love for me is unchanging. May I never fear or believe any contrary pronouncement on me.
Amen.

Day 21

AT AN ACCEPTABLE TIME

² For He says, "At an acceptable time I have listened to you, and on a day of salvation I have helped you."
2 Corinthians 6:2

Reflection

The Lord has you in mind, He has not forgotten you. It is His desire to see you happy and blessed. God doesn't loathe any of His creatures and He doesn't abandon any of His children. However, we cannot mount pressure on God. We cannot give Him ultimatums or compel Him to act according to our own timing. He says when the time is right, He will favour us. On the day He has planned, He will help us. Let us await Him in faith and joyful hope.

PRAYER

Lord Jesus, I surrender to your will and your plan. Give me faith and patience to wait joyfully for you and to one day receive the reward of what I have hoped for from you.
Amen.

Day 22

DO NOT TAKE MERCY FOR GRANTED

15 For He says to Moses, "I will have mercy on whom I have mercy, and I will have compassion on whom I have compassion."
Romans 9:15

Reflection

Mercy and grace are very important in the life of everyone. Mercy is not getting what we (our sins) deserve and grace is getting what we do not deserve. In both cases, it is to be treated better than we deserve. No one is to regard God's mercy towards them as a right. If God owes us mercy, it is no longer mercy but an obligation. Fortunately for us dear Child of God, the Lord is never tired of showing mercy to us if we are not tired of approaching Him. There is only one thing He asks of us - that we do not take His mercy for granted.

PRAYER

Lord Jesus, thank you for showing me mercy. May I also be an agent of your mercy in the world.
Amen.

Day 23

WE ARE A CHOSEN RACE

⁹ But you are a chosen race, a royal priesthood, a holy nation, God's own people, in order that you may proclaim the mighty acts of Him who called you out of darkness into His marvellous light.
1 Peter 2:9

Reflection

The honour that once exclusively belonged to the nation of Israel, is now extended to all Christians, their election, priesthood, their special place. We are special because in Jesus, we belong to God as His special people. Like priests we now have access to God - we are a Holy nation, which means we are under the government of God and we are His cherished possessions. Dear Child of God, we are privileged people. A Christian who understands this ought to be joyful, grateful and cheerful. When we know we are immensely blessed, we don't live like people returning from a funeral.

PRAYER

Lord Jesus, thank you for these privileges and great honour. May I celebrate each day, the joy of my heavenly riches through you.
Amen.

Day 24

THE INNOCENT ARE FORTUNATE

[10] Tell the innocent how fortunate they are,
for they shall eat the fruit of their labours.
Isaiah 3:10

Reflection

Dear Child of God, God cherishes and blesses innocence and uprightness. The world may think they are weak or insignificant but to God, they are very fortunate. The work of God says they shall eat the fruit of their labours. This means everyone shall reap the fruit of what they have sown. Those who sow innocence and righteousness shall reap blessings and favour from the Lord. Those who sow in the flesh, will reap according to what they have sown.

PRAYER

Lord Jesus, thank you for your Spirit and the grace through which I can live according to your will. Help me to sow uprightness and goodness so that I may reap what is good in time and eternity.
Amen.

Day 25

THE ANGELS, OUR PROTECTORS

²²My God sent His angel and shut the lions' mouths so that they would not hurt me, because I was found blameless before Him; and also before you, O king, I have done no wrong."
Daniel 6:22

Reflection

God's angels are encamped around those who fear and revere Him to rescue them. An instance of that is the rescue of Daniel. God sent His angel to shut the lions' mouths so that they would not hurt Daniel. Dear Child of God, God is a powerful protector; only what He wills can happen. Let us surrender to Him in every situation. If He wishes to protect us from something or give something to us, nothing can stop Him, but all things must be according to His will and wise providence.

PRAYER

Lord Jesus, nothing is impossible for you. I surrender to your plans for me. Do with me whatever you will.
Amen.

THE RIGHTEOUS IS BOLD

*The wicked flee when no one pursues, but
the righteous are as bold as a lion.*
Proverbs 28:1

Reflection

The wicked, because of their wickedness, are always living in fear. The sound of a shaken leaf frightens them. They are prompted by guilty conscience, fear of judgement, and fear of the consequence of their actions. They are suspicious of everyone. Fearing of being discovered, they fear where there is no cause for fear. Dear Child of God, for those who are godly and wise, there is nothing to fear; no fear of consequence, no qualm of conscience, no fear that their secret will be disclosed. They live in peace and with God's strength and they remain standing even when someone comes against them.

PRAYER

Lord Jesus, help me to shun anything that may condemn me to living in perpetual fear of the known and unknown.
Amen.

Day 27

SUFFERING IN THE FLESH

Since therefore Christ suffered in the flesh,
arm yourselves also with the same intention
(for whoever has suffered in the flesh has
finished with sin).
1 Peter 4:1

Reflection

Dear Child of God, we are called to have the same attitude as Christ, who suffered in the flesh. We must not gratify our flesh but practice self-denial and not allow the body to have mastery over us. When we deny ourselves, carry our cross and live not according to the dictate of the flesh but according to the principles of the Spirit, we are no longer under the dominion of sin.

PRAYER

Lord Jesus, help me to endure suffering as you did. Help me to mortify my flesh for the good of my spirit and to wage war with sin.
Amen.

Day 28

THE ALMIGHTY HAS PROMISED

35 Thus says the Lord, who gives the sun for light by day and the fixed order of the moon and the stars for light by night, who stirs up the sea so that its waves roar– the Lord of hosts is His name: 36 If this fixed order were ever to cease from my presence, says the Lord, then also the offspring of Israel would cease to be a nation before me forever.

Jeremiah 31:35-36

Reflection

God introduces Himself with a description of His incomparable power. He is the One who gives light. He created and controls the planets and stars. He rules over the storms and seas, and commands heavenly armies (LORD of hosts). The message from God is both powerful and plain. God will stop thinking of and dealing with Israel as a nation when the sun, moon, and stars stop giving light and when the sea stops roaring. As long as those things continue, God will regard Israel as a nation before Him forever. Dear Child of God, this promise is true for you because you are now part of God's people. For as long as star, moon and sun are still shining and even if they fail, God will continue to be gracious to us. His love is everlasting.

PRAYER

Lord Jesus, help me to grow in confidence that the Father loves me, and He will always care for me.
Amen.

Day 29

MY WORDS WILL NOT PASS AWAY

³¹ Heaven and earth will pass away, but my words will not pass away.
Mark 13:31

Reflection

What the Lord has promised you will never change. The truth of the Lord will endure from age to age. The Word of the Lord is timeless and timely, relevant for all people at all times. God doesn't utter vain words. His words are powerful and consistent. In God, there is no contradiction. When someone's words are true, unchanging, constant, non-contradictory and powerful, it means the person is reliable. Dear Child of God, you can stand on God's Word. He doesn't change, He is absolutely reliable.

PRAYER

Lord Jesus, thank you for your Word, which is trustworthy and reliable. May I base my confidence in the truth of your unchanging word.
Amen.

Day 30

THE WATCHTOWER

¹⁸ If I say to the wicked, "You shall surely die," and you give them no warning, or speak to warn the wicked from their wicked way, in order to save their life, those wicked persons shall die for their iniquity; but their blood I will require at your hand.

Ezekiel 3:18

Reflection

Dear Child of God, let no one say I am unconcerned about what's going on in the lives of others. The Lord doesn't want us to focus on the weaknesses of others, but often He reveals things to us so that we can help others to address them. Sometimes God wants to use us to help others to change and become better. Let us not be unconcerned about the spiritual wellbeing of others. When God sends us to warn others and we refuse to correct or help them, the Lord says we shall share in their guilt.

PRAYER

Lord Jesus, help me to always be mindful that I am my brother's keeper and I am meant to help him, at least within the bounds of charity, to become better and to live the life God has called him to.

Amen.

Day 31

GOD WILL SUPPLY YOUR NEEDS

*19 And my God will fully satisfy every need
of yours according to His riches in glory in
Christ Jesus.*
Philippians 4:19

Reflection

This is St. Paul's prayer for the Philippians; those who really supported God's service not out of their abundance but out of their sacrifice. St. Paul prayed that the Lord would supply their needs out of His riches in glory. Dear Child of God, take note that what God supplies is our needs not our greed or our wants. He supplies what we need to serve Him faithfully, what we need to be a blessing to others, what we need to live a decent and meaningful life. God will supply this according to His riches in glory. That's a staggering measure, there is no lack in God's riches in glory. However, it is not enough to claim the blessing; we should also learn and practice sacrificial generosity.

PRAYER

Lord Jesus, teach me to be truly generous and
to be counted worthy of your blessing.
Amen.

NOVEMBER

Day 1

THE SECOND DEATH

8 But as for the cowardly, the faithless, the polluted, the murderers, the fornicators, the sorcerers, the idolaters, and all liars, their place will be in the lake that burns with fire and sulphur, which is the second death.
Revelation 21:8

Reflection

People are often afraid of death. We are afraid of death for so many reasons, which include the pain of being separated from those we love, fear of the unknown and the uncertainty of what to expect after our death. Dear Child of God, the Word of God tells us that there are two deaths which we should be more afraid of. The first is spiritual death, which is caused by sin, and is when sin creates a distance between us and God who is source of our life and wellbeing. The second is eternal death which is eternal separation from God, the source of our existence and the one who can give eternal rest to our soul.

PRAYER

Lord Jesus, save me from spiritual and eternal death. May I glorify you by my life and by my death.
Amen.

Day 2

PROCLAIM THE MESSAGE

[1] In the presence of God and of Christ Jesus, who is to judge the living and the dead, and in view of His appearing and His kingdom, I solemnly urge you: [2] proclaim the message; be persistent whether the time is favourable or unfavourable; convince, rebuke, and encourage, with the utmost patience in teaching.
2 Timothy 4:1-2

Reflection

Dear Child of God, we have a message for the world. The message is that there is true and abundant life in Jesus. The message is that God loves everyone. The message is that there is hope in life for everyone and there is promise of eternal life for those who believe. We have a message that God bestows forgiveness and peace, and sinners should repent and embrace a new life. This is our message. We have a mandate to proclaim this to the world. The world may not want to hear it, but it is what everyone needs to hear. So let us proclaim this message and teach it with patience and persistence, not just by words but the example of a good life.

PRAYER

Lord Jesus, give me the strength to proclaim your message of hope to the world.
Amen.

Day 3

NAME ABOVE ALL NAMES

*⁹ Therefore God also highly exalted Him
and gave Him the name that is above every
name.*
Philippians 2:9

Reflection

The name of Jesus is a powerful name. When we invoke the name of Jesus, we invoke His power and presence. Dear Child of God, revere this name, believe in it. Trust in the power of that name, pray through that powerful name, glorify that name, call upon that name for salvation and deliverance. There is no other name by which we can be saved except in that name.

PRAYER

Lord Jesus, I believe in the power of your name. As I revere and invoke your name, may you break every chain and yoke that might be in my life and in my family.
Amen.

THE NAME OF THE LORD IS A STRONG TOWER

10 The name of the Lord is a strong tower;
the righteous run into it and are safe.
Proverbs 18:10

Reflection

In the Lord, there is salvation for every one of us. When we run to the Lord, trusting in His name and character, we find a strong tower. Within these walls, the sharpest arrows cannot touch us, we are preserved from external troubles, we are in a place of protection, mercy and refuge. It is through that name of the Lord that David conquered Goliath, and it is through that name dear Child of God, that no Goliath of life will overpower you.

PRAYER

Lord Jesus, I run to you for refuge. May I feel protected under the shadow of your wings and through the saving power of your most holy name.
Amen.

Day 5

THE LOVER OF MONEY

10 The lover of money will not be satisfied with money; nor the lover of wealth, with gain. This also is vanity. 11 When goods increase, those who eat them increase; and what gain has their owner but to see them with his eyes?
Ecclesiastes 5:10-11

Reflection

Dear Child of God, money is good and valuable in life, but we must not place more value on money than it deserves. There are things that are more important than money and we must not lose sight of them in our search for money. Our faith, our family, our conscience, our salvation, our integrity - all these are not for sale and they must never be compromised because of wealth. Money is temporal and so is its value. Money is not to be worshipped but to be used wisely and pursued with caution and honesty. It will be a bad bargain to jeopardise our souls in the bid to increase gain; contentment is key.

PRAYER

Lord Jesus, help me to appreciate what you have given me and never offend you in my longing for riches.
Amen.

Day 6

EAT MY FLESH

⁵⁴ Those who eat my flesh and drink my blood have eternal life, and I will raise them up on the last day.
John 6:54

Reflection

Dear Child of God, Jesus invites us to eat His flesh and drink His blood. In the Holy Eucharist, Jesus has made Himself present to us as real food for our souls. He wants to nourish our souls with Himself and dwell with us sacramentally. Let us always be grateful to the Lord for the gift of Himself. Let us make every effort to receive Jesus worthily and with sincere reverence. As we receive Jesus in Communion, let us remember to be bread broken for the world too.

PRAYER

Lord Jesus, thank you for giving yourself to me in Holy Communion. May I always receive you with utmost reverence and joy.
Amen.

Day 7

I CHOSE YOU

*¹⁶You did not choose me, but I chose you.
And I appointed you to go and bear fruit,
fruit that will last, so that the Father will
give you whatever you ask Him in my
name.*
John 15:16

Reflection

Dear Child of God, God chose us from all eternity. He chose us in Christ. He chose us for holiness, revelation, salvation and for mission. We are chosen before the foundation of the world to be holy, to have a knowledge of God's will and the mystery of salvation. We are chosen to be saved and to bear fruit in the world. As we rejoice in our election and privileges, let us not lose sight of our mandate, which is to bear fruit, fruit that will last.

PRAYER

Lord Jesus, thank you for calling and choosing me. May I not be barren spiritually but bear fruits for you in this world, fruits that will last. Amen.

SALVATION FOR THOSE WHO TRUST

[32] Then everyone who calls on the name of the Lord shall be saved; for in Mount Zion and in Jerusalem there shall be those who escape, as the Lord has said, and among the survivors shall be those whom the Lord calls.

Joel 2:32

Reflection

This is a mighty promise dear Child of God - there is salvation for anyone who trusts in the Lord, who calls upon Him. You cannot perish while trusting in the Lord. No one calls on the Lord and is rejected by the Lord. God will not forfeit His promise, His mercy, His character of love. Let us keep in mind that salvation is not in any false god, the god of our opinion and imagination. Salvation comes from the Lord who made heaven and earth.

PRAYER

Lord Jesus, may I find salvation and strength in your name and in your promise.
Amen.

Day 9

LIVING HOLY AND GODLY LIVES

Since everything will be destroyed in this
way, what kind of people ought you to be?
You ought to live holy and godly lives.
2 Peter 3:11

Reflection

Dear Child of God, the Lord has made us for Himself.
He created us for His own purpose and pleasure. He
wants to be at the centre of our lives. This is what a
godly life means – a life in which God is at the centre,
a life that focuses on God, that places God above
everything, that honours God in every situation. It is a
life that seeks to praise and glorify God. This is how we
ought to live. Those who live this way are honoured by
God and saved for a glorious eternity with Him.

PRAYER

Lord Jesus, help me to put you in front, in front
of everyone. Be at the centre of my life, and may
my life revolve around you alone.
Amen.

BE ON YOUR GUARD AGAINST GREED

[15] And He said to them, "Take care! Be on your guard against all kinds of greed; for one's life does not consist in the abundance of possessions."
Luke 12:15

Reflection

Dear Child of God, heed the Lord's warning today and guard against all forms of greed. Greed is an intense, selfish and inordinate desire for something - money, privilege, power, position, pleasure, possession. Simplicity and contentment are very great virtues. Greed makes us vulnerable and plunges us into serious temptation. Keep the words of Jesus in mind - one's happiness doesn't consist in abundance of possession.

PRAYER

Lord Jesus, free my heart from inordinate love or attachment to anything. May my heart be free to love you as my supreme good and cause of happiness.
Amen.

Day 11

IT IS NOT BY MIGHT

He said to me, "This is the word of the Lord to Zerubbabel: Not by might, nor by power, but by my spirit, says the Lord of hosts.
Zechariah 4:6

Reflection

This is the Word of the Lord to Zerubbabel. Zerubbabel was the civic leader of Jerusalem and had the responsibility to finish the work of rebuilding the temple. The work had stalled, and Zerubbabel needed encouragement to carry on the work. The Lord reminded Zerubbabel that it is "not by the resources of many or one, but by My Spirit." That is, it will not be by your cleverness, your ability or your physical strength that the temple will be rebuilt, but by the Spirit of God. Dear Child of God, this message holds true for us. Let us not over rely on our strength, skill and ideas. The most important resource for doing God's work and excelling in His purpose is the Holy Spirit.

PRAYER

Lord Jesus, open the eyes of my mind to understand that it is only by the power of the Holy Spirit that I can succeed in fulfilling God's plan and mission.
Amen.

Day 12

NOT BY BREAD ALONE

⁴ But He answered, "It is written, 'One does not live by bread alone, but by every word that comes from the mouth of God.'"

Matthew 4:4

Reflection

Physical food is very important and necessary for the sustenance of natural life, however, the human person is not just corporeal, but also spiritual. Hence, physical food is necessary but not sufficient. Since the human person is body and soul, they need the nourishment of the soul too and it is the Word of God and the bread of eternal salvation (Holy Eucharist) that strengthen the soul.

Dear Child of God, do not feed your body and neglect your soul. Do not eat well physically and have a starving soul. Each time you receive the Eucharist in a state of grace and meditate on the Word of God, you give your soul a pleasant treat.

PRAYER

Lord Jesus, thank you for your Word and your Body. Let these provide nourishment to my soul always.

Amen.

Day 13

THE LAW OF THE LORD IS PERFECT

⁷ The law of the Lord is perfect, reviving the soul; the decrees of the Lord are sure, making wise the simple.
Psalm 19:7

Reflection

One of the surest places we can learn and gain great wisdom is through the study of God's Word. In the Bible, we have access to words of wisdom and powerful counsel to revive our soul, order our lives, reshape our perspective and better our existence. Dear Child of God, do you wish to grow in knowledge and wisdom? Open your Bible and ask the Holy Spirit to fill you with wisdom as you reflect on the power of God's Word.

PRAYER

Lord Jesus, fill me with wisdom as I reflect on the power of your love made known through your saving Word.
Amen.

HIS NAME IS JESUS

21 She will bear a son, and you are to name Him Jesus, for He will save His people from their sins.
Matthew 1:21c

Reflection

The name of Jesus means the Lord saves. Jesus is a Saviour. He saves us from the dominion of sin. He saves us from the just wrath of God. He saves us from the devil and all his evil spirits. He saves us from meaningless life, and He saves us from our fears and worries. Jesus saves us from eternal damnation.

Dear Child of God, let us discover in Jesus not just a Saviour but a friend. He wants to hold us and walk more closely with us. The more we open our hearts to Him and go deeper in our friendship with Him, the more we experience the joy and assurance of salvation.

PRAYER

Lord Jesus, thank you for being my Saviour. May I come to you also as a friend; yes, as a grateful friend.
Amen.

330

Day 15

PEACE FOR THOSE WHO TRUST

³ Those of steadfast mind you keep in peace
- in peace because they trust in you.
Isaiah 26:3

Reflection

Dear Child of God, the Lord keeps those who steadfastly trust in Him in perfect peace. Those whose eyes are fixed on Him look not at the threat or danger around them; they do not magnify their problem above their God. They look to the Lord and ponder on His greatness. This is the secret of perfect peace. When we focus on our problems and we lose sight of God's greatness, we relinquish our peace.

PRAYER

Lord Jesus, may my eyes be always on you and in this, may I find peace amidst the world's uncertainty and distress.
Amen.

CHERISH NO INIQUITY IN YOUR HEART

*¹⁸ If I had cherished iniquity in my heart,
the Lord would not have listened.*
Psalm 66:18

Reflection

Dear Child of God, your heart is a holy place. It is a place of worship, it is the throne of the Most High, a temple of the Holy Spirit. Do not cherish iniquity in your heart. Do not open the door of your heart to sin. Do not accommodate anything that can defile God's Holy place. A prayer that proceeds from a God-fearing heart avails much.

PRAYER

Lord Jesus, purify my heart of all that is unworthy of you. I lay my heart as an altar before you, and I worship you in the temple of my heart.
Amen.

Day 17

PRAY WITHOUT DOUBTING

²² Jesus answered them, "Have faith in God. ²³ Truly I tell you, if you say to this mountain, 'Be taken up and thrown into the sea,' and if you do not doubt in your heart but believe that what you say will come to pass, it will be done for you.

Mark 11:22b-23

Reflection

Sometimes when we pray, we doubt whether God is listening and whether He will answer us. Sometimes we pray and yet we do not expect an answer. Many people pray and they are very surprised when God answers. It is as if they weren't expecting Him to answer. As for you dear Child of God, keep in mind that faith is the key to the heart of God. When you pray, believe that God is there listening to you. Believe that God is able to answer you. Believe that your prayers are heard and will be answered in God's way and in His time. No prayer of faith is ever wasted, and when we truly believe, we generously receive.

PRAYER

Lord Jesus, I trust in you. May I receive from you what I ask with faith.

Amen.

Day 18

PUT ON THE ARMOUR OF LIGHT

12 the night is far gone, the day is near. Let us then lay aside the works of darkness and put on the armour of light.
Romans 13:12

Reflection

Dear Child of God, we are called to lay aside the works of darkness and put on the armour of light. We must cast off the rags of sin before we can put on the robe of Christ. We must renounce the practices and habits of sin, because we cannot wear religion as an overall on top of old sins. We have to lay aside something to put on something new. The works of darkness are characterised as drunkenness, revelry, licentiousness and lust, strife and envy. Those are no longer appropriate for Christians who have come out of the night into God's light.

PRAYER

Lord Jesus, help me to lay aside the garment of sin and put on Christ who is light and truth. Amen.

Day 19

RENOUNCE IMPIETY AND WORLDLY PASSION

*¹¹ For the grace of God has appeared,
bringing salvation to all, ¹² training us to
renounce impiety and worldly passions, and
in the present age to live lives that are self-
controlled, upright, and godly...*
Titus 2:11-12

Reflection

Dear Child of God, we have all received salvation
through grace and through the power of this same
saving grace, we are all called to renounce impiety and
worldly passions. Our lives must be lived in self-
control, uprightness and godliness. Self-control in
regard to ourselves, is living uprightly in regard to
people around us, and we must live godly lives, in
regard to God.

PRAYER

Lord Jesus help me by the power of your grace
to live a life of self-control. Help me to be
upright and godly.
Amen.

ZEALOUS FOR GOOD DEEDS

14 He it is who gave Himself for us that He might redeem us from all iniquity and purify for Himself a people of His own who are zealous for good deeds.
Titus 2:14

Reflection

Dear Child of God, we are purchased by Christ' blood and redeemed from iniquity so that we may live with zeal. Zeal for what? Zeal for God, zeal for righteousness, zeal to do His will, zeal to bring others to the knowledge of the truth. A child of God must always be zealous for God and for the things of God.

PRAYER

Lord Jesus, fill me with knowledge and zeal for righteousness, for good works and for the salvation of the souls of those around me. Amen.

Day 21

ABIDE IN ME

⁴ Abide in me as I abide in you. Just as the branch cannot bear fruit by itself unless it abides in the vine, neither can you unless you abide in me.

John 15:4

Reflection

Dear Child of God, Christ is the reason for our glory. He is the cause of all that is good in us. It is through Him that we shine, and it is His beauty in us that is attracting people's acclaim and admiration. Let us hold Him firmly. Let us declare that we are nothing without Him and let us be deeply rooted in Him and never succumb to anything that threatens to separate us from Him. Without Him, there is no form or comeliness in us. Independent of Him, we are objects of pity.

PRAYER

Lord Jesus, may I remain rooted in you so that I may continue to flourish and bear fruit and reflect your glory.
Amen.

THE LORD SURROUNDS HIS PEOPLE

²As the mountains surround Jerusalem, so the Lord surrounds His people, from this time on and forevermore.
Psalm 125:2

Reflection

Dear Child of God, the Lord promises to surround you, just as mountain surrounds Jerusalem. Keep in mind that you are never alone or forlorn. You are not a garden without a wall. The Lord says His power will surround you. The Lord surrounds you for protection. He surrounds you as a shield. He surrounds you for deliverance. Claim this for yourself. I am surrounded by God's loving presence, and when I am surrounded by God, it matters not what is around me, because the One who surrounds me is able to protect me.

PRAYER

Lord Jesus, thank you for your angels all around me. May I rejoice to receive their help and protection.
Amen.

Day 23

THE STATE OF YOUR HEART

⚜

²²... adultery, avarice, wickedness, deceit, licentiousness, envy, slander, pride, folly. ²³ All these evil things come from within, and they defile a person."
Mark 7:23

Reflection

Dear Child of God, the state of your heart is very important. God is very interested in what goes on within you. God is honoured when we come before Him with clean hands and pure hearts. Let us therefore surrender ourselves to the purifying power of the Holy Spirit, to purge us of anything that can pollute our hearts - vices like sexual impurity, deceit, envy, pride, unforgiveness, avarice, hatred and the like.

PRAYER

Lord Jesus, may your Spirit purify my heart from all corruption of vices. Sacred Heart of Jesus, make my heart like unto thine.
Amen.

JUST AS YOUR HEAVENLY FATHER

⁴⁸ Be perfect, therefore, as your heavenly Father is perfect.
Matthew 5:48

Reflection

Dear Child of God, do not compare your righteousness with others. Do not make anyone your measure of holiness. Let our Heavenly Father be your standard. Aspire to love, be kind, be merciful, be forgiving, be humble, and be patient like Jesus. How is that possible? If the Spirit who is in Jesus is in you, you will be able to live like Him.

PRAYER

Lord Jesus, pour out your Spirit on me; may you be formed in me.
Amen.

DO NOT PUT THE LORD TO THE TEST

⁹ We must not put Christ to the test, as some of them did, and were destroyed by serpents.
1 Corinthians 10:9

Reflection

Dear Child of God, God is to be trusted and not to be tested. Let us be careful not to put the Lord to the test in any way. We test the Lord when we continue wilfully and obstinately in sin and we presume His mercy. We put the Lord to the test when we are wicked and unkind to others. We put the Lord to the test when we give him conditions or ultimatums. We put the Lord to the test when we wilfully refuse to obey His voice. We put the Lord to the test if we foolishly plunge ourselves into unnecessary danger and expect Him to deliver us miraculously.

PRAYER

Lord Jesus, forgive me for the times I might have put you to the test. Teach me to trust and to obey, for there is no other way to be happy in you.
Amen.

THOSE WHO SEEK THE LORD

The young lions suffer want and hunger, but those who seek the Lord lack no good thing.
Psalm 34:10

Reflection

The Lord our God is a great provider. He cares about us His children. Here is a promise we can hold unto - He says strong lions may suffer want and go hungry, but He will be a great provider to us. Dear Child of God, God takes special care to supply our needs, even through extraordinary means. However, sometimes God denies us some things we crave for, not out of wickedness but mercy. When we ask for snakes instead of bread, He might deny us the supply instead of granting it.

PRAYER

Lord Jesus, I confess that you are a great provider and I confess that you know my needs. May you supply according to your riches in glory.
Amen.

Day 27

THE RACE IS NOT TO THE SWIFT

*11 Again I saw that under the sun the race
is not to the swift, nor the battle to the
strong, nor bread to the wise, nor riches to
the intelligent, nor favour to the skilful; but
time and chance happen to them* all.
Ecclesiastes 9:11

Reflection

Favour is greater than labour. Our effort is very important for success, but we must know that everything doesn't depend on our efforts, vision, creativity, intelligence, smartness, preparedness or stamina. Dear Child of God, after you have made effort, acknowledge the Lord and ask Him to crown your effort with success. The Lord's blessing is more certain to bring success than any human effort can.

PRAYER

Lord Jesus, I acknowledge that your favour and blessing are more important than my effort. May I rest more in you than in myself and my effort.

Amen.

OBEDIENCE IS THE PROOF OF LOVE

15 If you love me, you will keep my commandments.
John 14:15

Reflection

Dear Child of God, the most important indication of the love of God is not that we come to Church, we work in the Church, we say long prayers and that we are members of many societies. The most significant indication of love of God is obedience. Spirituality is obedience to the Lord and charity towards others. Am I obedient to the Lord? Do I do His will, or do I just call Him "Lord! Lord!" and then go my way.

PRAYER

Lord Jesus, help me to truly love and honour you, not with my lips alone but with a heart that obeys you.
Amen.

Day 29

IF I FORGET JERUSALEM

*If I forget you, O Jerusalem, let my right-hand
wither! Let my tongue cling to the roof of my
mouth, if I do not remember you, if I do not set
Jerusalem above my highest joy.*

Psalm 137:5-6

Reflection

The singer vowed he would never forget God's holy
city and gave a curse upon himself if he did. The godly,
though in exile, could not forget Jerusalem and
everything it stands for: covenant, temple, presence,
kingship of God, atonement, worship. He vowed never
to forget God's promise and to persevere waiting for
the moment of redemption. He vowed to prize the
restoration of Jerusalem above all his joys. Dear Child
of God, let us also not forget the blessings of God in
our lives, the sacrifice of Jesus for us on the cross, the
faith in which we were baptised and saved, the values
taught to us in the Church, the Sacraments which give
us grace. Let us not let these slip away from us as we
journey through life. Let us not, in pursuit of a desired
future or worldly advantage, lose the things that should
be most important and definitive in our lives.

PRAYER

Lord Jesus, may I not forget or lose those treasures
that God has bestowed upon me. May I prize the
salvation of my soul above all my joys.
Amen.

Day 30

GOD SEES YOUR GOOD DEEDS

⁴ He stared at him in terror and said, "What is it, Lord?" He answered, "Your prayers and your alms have ascended as a memorial before God."
Acts 10:4

Reflection

Dear Child of God, people may not take note of your kindness and good deeds. People may not see your effort. People may not acknowledge your sacrifice, and you may not be recognised as extraordinary among people. But one thing is sure; your good deeds, your kind works, your charity, and your works of mercy will never go unnoticed and unrewarded by God. In the long run, it is the Lord's reward that is most important.

PRAYER

Lord Jesus, help me to dedicate my life to good works whether appreciated by others or not. May all I do be done for God's sake and in gratitude for His love.
Amen.

DECEMBER

JESUS IS THE WAY

⁶ *Jesus said to him, "I am the way, and the truth, and the life. No one comes to the Father except through me."*

John 14:6

Reflection

Dear Child of God, this is a message we must constantly meditate on and share with others. Following Jesus is the way to peace, joy, everlasting happiness. In Jesus, we find truth that liberates.

It is in Him that we have abundance of life in time and eternity. He gives us access to God and confidence in God's presence. Let no one deceive themselves that outside of Jesus, there is another way to truth and life.

PRAYER

Lord Jesus, help me to keep believing in you. Help me to follow and surrender to you. Amen.

Day 2

THE LORD ANSWERED JABEZ

Jabez called on the God of Israel, saying,
"Oh that you would bless me and enlarge
my border, and that your hand might be
with me, and that you would keep me from
hurt and harm!" And God granted what he
asked.

1 Chronicles 4:10

Reflection

Jabez called on God to bless, protect and enlarge his border and the Lord granted him his petitions. God listens to prayers and He is a giver of good gifts. Dear Child of God, just as Jabez asked for blessing, protection and increase, let us ask God also for faith greater than whatever crises we are going through, wisdom to govern our lives and deal with difficult cases and people and for the grace to accept God's will without grumbling or complaining.

PRAYER

Lord Jesus, I call upon you today. I pray for greater faith, increased wisdom and grace of joyful resignation to your will.
Amen.

Day 3

WE HAVE AN ADVOCATE
WITH THE FATHER

[1] My little children, I am writing these things to you so that you may not sin. But if anyone does sin, we have an advocate with the Father, Jesus Christ the righteous; [2] and He is the atoning sacrifice for our sins, and not for ours only but also for the sins of the whole world.
1 John 2:1-2

Reflection

Dear Child of God, we have a high priest in heaven, a mediator. He is the Lamb of God who took away our sins and now He sits at God's right hand, still interceding for us and the whole world. Let us not allow sin and guilt to put us in bondage. Let us not helplessly wait for punishment of sin. We can obtain mercy by bringing our sins to the foot of the cross and lifting our eyes to Jesus for mercy.

PRAYER

Lord Jesus, I have confidence in you and in you I place my hope of mercy. Your treasury of compassion is inexhaustible; may I never despair of mercy or surrender to sin.
Amen.

Day 4

EXALTATION THROUGH HUMILITY

.... for all who exalt themselves will be humbled, but all who humble themselves will be exalted.
Luke 18:14b

Reflection

Humility is the glory of a soul. Grace works more freely and abundantly in a humble soul. A humble soul acknowledges God and understands that it is nothing outside of God. The motivation of a humble heart is not the flaunting of the self but to see that which is praised and glorified. Dear Child of God, God looks for humility in us. He requires it to show us mercy, to partner with us in massive projects, to lift us up and to dispense His graces to others through us.

PRAYER

Lord Jesus, meek and humble of heart, make my heart like yours. May I have the same mindset that you have when you left your glory to take our poor human condition.
Amen.

Day 5

HE IS ABLE TO DO MORE

20 Now to Him who by the power at work within us is able to accomplish abundantly far more than all we can ask or imagine.
Ephesians 3:20

Reflection

God is able to do more than we can ever ask for or imagine. God is beyond our power of prediction and He gives us even more than our expectation. He works in ways we may not see. He makes a way where there seems to be no way. He brings to reality what is beyond our comprehension. He gives what we do not deserve, and He shows mercy more than we can beg for. He is just a good God. Dear Child of God, celebrate God's goodness and praise Him for His surpassing benevolence. No matter your circumstance, do not stop saying "God is good all the time."

PRAYER

Lord Jesus, you are good, and your ways are perfect. May your goodness and kindness always follow me.
Amen.

Day 6

IN HIM IS LIFE

⁴ ... in him was life, and the life was the
light of all people.
John 1:4

Reflection

St. John invites us to a deep reflection on the person of Jesus. He is the source of all life - not only biological life, but the very principle of life. The ancient Greek word translated life is 'zoe', which means "the life principle," not 'bios', which is mere biological life. That power which creates life and maintains all else in existence is in Jesus. This life is the light of men. It isn't that the Word "contains" life and light; He is life and light. Dear Child of God, without Jesus, we are dead and in darkness. Let us thank God for light and life in us and let us bring this light and life to others through our words and examples.

PRAYER

Lord Jesus, in you is life and light. Save me from living in the darkness of the grave.
Amen.

Day 7

BE HOSPITABLE

*⁹ Be hospitable to one another without
complaining.*
1 Peter 4:9

Reflection

Dear Child of God, hospitality is a great virtue. The
Lord calls us to practice and show this to others. Let us
be loving and welcoming to others, spreading the
fragrance of God's goodness. Let us pray for a big heart
that embraces all but also a discerning spirit that is able
to see beyond pretence and appearance.

PRAYER

Lord Jesus, help me to be loving and hospitable.
Teach me to be discerning so that I don't make
regrettable mistakes.
Amen.

THE WORKS THAT I DO

~~~~~~~

³⁶ But I have a testimony greater than
John's. The works that the Father has given
me to complete, the very works that I am
doing, testify on my behalf that the Father
has sent me.
John 5:36

Reflection

Dear Child of God, the work we do should be our testimony, our evidence, our warrant that we belong to Jesus and are working for His kingdom. When I reconcile friends, counsel the doubtful, instruct the ignorant in the ways of God, when I am committed to the corporal and spiritual works of mercy and promote the work of evangelization, I testify by my work that I work for God and I am on the assignment of the Father. Let us not allow ourselves to be used by the devil for His assignment and purpose.

PRAYER

Lord Jesus, let my works testify that I am all yours.
Amen.

HE IS WORTHY TO BE PRAISED

³ I call upon the Lord, who is worthy to be praised, so I shall be saved from my enemies.
Psalm 18:3

Reflection

Dear Child of God, in sickness or health, in abundance or scarcity, alone or in the midst of others, when we have lost someone dear to us or when a new member is added to our family, when the sun rises or when it sets, the Lord is worthy to be praised. His mercy endures forever, His greatness cannot be measured, His holiness is incomparable, His Power is incontestable. Great are His works, they are marvellous in our sight. May His praise never cease on our lips.

PRAYER

Lord Jesus, you are worthy of praise. Help me to worship you in Spirit and in truth as you deserve.
Amen.

Day 10

MY GLORY I GIVE TO NO OTHER

⁸I am the Lord, that is my name; my glory I give to no other, nor my praise to idols.
Isaiah 42:8

Reflection

Dear Child of God, our God is the Lord, He is the Almighty. He is greater than everyone. He is far above all spirits, sovereignty and power. No god can be compared to Him in might and glory. To Him alone be all the glory. Let us not give to any human being, any spirit or idol, the glory that is due to God alone.

PRAYER

Lord Jesus, I give you glory, and I honour you. Above and beside you, there is no other. To you alone be my worship and adoration.
Amen.

Day 11

BE GENEROUS

38 ...give, and it will be given to you. A good measure, pressed down, shaken together, running over, will be put into your lap; for the measure you give will be the measure you get back.
Luke 6:38

Reflection

Dear Child of God, be generous and giving. Do not merely ask and receive from God without giving to others. When you want to give to others, give what is good, acceptable and helpful. Every giving is sowing, and we shall reap what we sow. Just as the Lord has been kind to us, let us become a channel of God's blessing to others.

PRAYER

Lord Jesus, make me a channel of your blessing to others. May I not hoard your blessing but transmit to others what I have received out of your gracious love.
Amen.

Day 12

MAY HE ANSWER YOU

¹ The Lord answer you in the day of trouble! The name of the God of Jacob protect you! ² May He send you help from the sanctuary, and give you support from Zion.

Psalm 20:1-2

Reflection

Dear Child of God, in the days of joy, praise God. In the days of need, call on Him. In the days of adversity, trust in Him. May He answer you in the days of trouble, and may you experience the power of His name. May He send you help from the sanctuary and support from Zion. Whenever God blesses or helps you out of trouble, do not forget to always thank Him and testify to His greatness in the assembly of His faithful.

PRAYER

Lord Jesus, in you I place my hope. May the troubles of life not overwhelm me. May I find safety in you and may I boldly testify to your power.
Amen.

Day 13

LET YOUR LIGHT SHINE

⚜

¹⁶ In the same way, let your light shine before others, so that they may see your good works and give glory to your Father in heaven.

Matthew 5:1

Reflection

Dear Child of God, you are a light in the world. We are to show others good examples, instruct them in the ways of God and lead them on the path of truth, justice and holiness. We must constantly be engaged in good works, not to gain ourselves recognition or good name, renown or reputation, but for His own glory. Our joy must be to see Him and Him alone honoured and glorified.

PRAYER

Lord Jesus, help me to honour you by a good life and glorify you by good works.
Amen.

Day 14

BEWARE OF HYPOCRISY

*¹Meanwhile, when the crowd gathered by the
thousands, so that they trampled on one
another, He began to speak first to His
disciples, "Beware of the yeast of the
Pharisees, that is, their hypocrisy. ² Nothing is
covered up that will not be uncovered, and
nothing secret that will not become known.*
Luke 12:1-2

Reflection

Dear Child of God, the Lord warns us against
hypocrisy. Hypocrisy is acting to be righteous when we
are not and when we are not even intending to be. It is
pretending to be who we are not. Hypocrisy depends
on concealment. Jesus tells us to desist from it because
we can only hide from others and not from God. More
so, everything hidden will one day be revealed. If there
is anything you do not want anyone to discover about
you, if there is anything that can put you to shame
when revealed, desist from it.

PRAYER

Lord Jesus, help me to be sincere in my walk
with you and to be authentic to others.
Amen.

WALK BEFORE ME AND
BE BLAMELESS

[1] When Abram was ninety-nine years old, the Lord appeared to Abram, and said to him, "I am God Almighty; walk before me, and be blameless. [2] And I will make my covenant between me and you and will make you exceedingly numerous."

Genesis 17:1-2

Reflection

God renewed His covenant with Abraham. He promised to bless Abraham exceedingly. All He requested from Abraham was to walk with Him and be blameless. Dear Child of God, we are children of the covenant. We are Abraham's children but more importantly, we are covered by the New Covenant, established through the blood of Jesus. What God required of Abraham, He also requires of us - to walk with Him in trust and to avoid anything that is blameworthy and displeasing in God's sight. Let us ask the Father through the Son and by the power of the Holy Spirit, to give us grace to walk humbly with Him and avoid what will lead to our being blamed.

PRAYER

Lord Jesus, stretch out your hand and hold mine and allow me to walk closer with you; this is all I ask for.

Amen.

Day 16

DISOBEDIENCE IS REBELLION

―――――――――

23 For rebellion is no less a sin than divination,
and stubbornness is like iniquity and idolatry.
Because you have rejected the Word of the Lord,
He has also rejected you from being king.
1 Samuel 15:23

Reflection

Samuel denounced Saul for disobeying the voice of God and carrying out his own desires. Dear Child of God, disobedience to God is a sort of rebellion. The language of disobedience is "Lord, I know what you want, I know what you have commanded, but I choose to do what I want. I know this is displeasing to you, but I will do it nonetheless, even though you ask me not to do it. But doing it will make me feel good and that's all I care." Is this not rebellion? To know what God commands and forbids and yet act as if we don't care? It is this rebellion that brought Saul from grace to grass. Let us learn from Saul and be wise.

PRAYER

Lord Jesus, you are an example of perfect obedience. Help me to be obedient to the Father even unto death.
Amen.

Day 17

TELL NO ONE

⁹ As they were coming down the mountain, He ordered them to tell no one about what they had seen, until after the Son of Man had risen from the dead.

Mark 9:9

Reflection

The disciples had witnessed a great miracle, something exceedingly marvellous. When we have such an experience, our immediate impulse would be to look for someone to share with and talk to. But Jesus charged His disciples to tell no one about this. Dear Child of God, there are times when we need to learn to keep quiet. The Bible even urges us to be slow to speak. It is not everything we know, see, dream of, plan, think about, hear that we must say. Let us learn to keep quiet when we are unsure of something. Let us learn to keep quiet instead of speaking ill of someone or responding to insult with an insult. Let us learn to keep quiet when it is someone else' secret we are about to let out. Let us learn to keep quiet if what wants to come out of our mouth is boastful, untrue, impure or misleading.

PRAYER

Lord Jesus, keep a sentry at the door of my lips and save me from free speaking idle words. May my words be true, edifying and seasoned with grace.
Amen.

Day 18

DO YOU ALSO WISH TO GO AWAY?

⁶⁶ Because of this many of His disciples turned back and no longer went about with Him. ⁶⁷ So Jesus asked the twelve, "Do you also wish to go away?" ⁶⁸ Simon Peter answered Him, "Lord, to whom can we go? You have the words of eternal life.

John 6:66-68

Reflection

Jesus discouraged every material and earthly motive for following Him. He preached about His flesh being a spiritual food and His blood a spiritual drink, and because of this, many people stopped following Him. They took an exception to His teaching. It is not new that some people are today turning their backs to the Church, to Jesus, to faith, to the Gospel, to Christian values. Some people turned their backs to Jesus and stopped following Him. Dear Child of God, Jesus turned to the disciples and He turns to us to ask, "do you also wish to go away?" Let us declare like St. Peter, "Lord, you are all I have, you are my only hope. On you I rest, in you, I place my confidence, I have no one else to go to apart from you. I accept whatever you say, give, will, plan or allocate to me."

PRAYER

Lord Jesus, you have the words of eternal life and I will cling to you forever.
Amen.

HEAVEN IS OUR TRUE HOME

²⁴ I will take you from the nations, and gather you from all the countries, and bring you into your own land.
Ezekiel 36:24

Reflection

God promised to bring His people from the nations where they were exiled and resettle them on their land. Dear Child of God, the Bible says that we have no permanent abode in this world. Our homeland is in heaven. As long as we are in this world, we are earth's exile. Heaven is our true home. Let us never lose sight of our homeland. Let us live in this world as people who look forward to their own eternal city. Let us serve God faithfully and joyfully in this world so that one day we shall be harvested from this world into the eternal happiness with the Father in our true native land.

PRAYER

Lord Jesus, may the hope of heaven inspire me to live a good life on earth. May I never lose sight of my true and lasting home.
Amen.

Day 20

I WAITED PATIENTLY

*¹ I waited patiently for the Lord; He
inclined to me and heard my cry.*
Psalm 40:1

Reflection

Dear Child of God, in our relationship with God, patience is a very important virtue. We cannot rush God or dictate time and manner. He is never desperate as we are, neither does He rush. He is never in haste, but He is never late. He is always on time and shows up at the best time. Lack of patience is one of the reasons we make terrible mistakes in life. We are too quick to give up on God, on life, on others, on ourselves, and hence we make decisions, take steps and initiate actions that we eventually regret. Let us beg the Holy Spirit to produce in us the fruit of earnest and diligent patience until the Lord inclines to us and hears our cry.

PRAYER

Lord Jesus, I beg for patience. Calm my anxious spirit and teach me to wait in faith and joyful hope for what you have promised.
Amen.

HE TOUCHED THE UNTOUCHABLE

² and there was a leper who came to Him and knelt before Him, saying, "Lord, if you choose, you can make me clean." ³ He stretched out His hand and touched him, saying, "I do choose. Be made clean!" Immediately his leprosy was cleansed.

Matthew 8:2-3

Reflection

Dear Child of God, we see the power of Jesus over sickness well demonstrated. However, there is something more; we see the mercy of God. Jesus stretched out His hand and touched the untouchable. Mercy moves us to touch the untouchable, to see the unrecognised, to love the unlovable. Mercy moves us to act to help even those undeserving. This healing of the leper is a token demonstration of God's mercy. Jesus still wants to touch people in misery. He wants to use you. If you feel touched by His mercy, let His mercy touch someone through you.

PRAYER

Lord Jesus, touch my heart so that I may be moved to compassion to touch others too. Amen.

Day 22

RESIST THE DEVIL

Submit yourselves therefore to God. Resist the devil, and he will flee from you.
James 4:7

Reflection

Dear Child of God, the Lord has given you power and authority to be able to stand against the devil, his deception, temptation, machination and attacks. How do we resist the devil? We resist the devil by the power of solid faith. We resist the devil by the knowledge of God's Word and standing on the promises of God. We resist the devil by the power in the name of Jesus. We resist the devil by the boldness that the Holy Spirit gives. We resist the devil by the power in praising God, by loving God above everything, by self-denial, by holiness of life, by the victory on the cross and by the power of the blood. Let us set the devil running back in confusion each time he hastens to deceive us.

PRAYER

Lord Jesus, by the power of your name and through your victory on the cross, I claim victory over the devil and his agents.
Amen.

DRAW NEAR TO GOD

*Draw near to God, and He will draw near
to you. Cleanse your hands, you sinners,
and purify your hearts, you double-minded.*
James 4:8

Reflection

Dear Child of God, what a powerful counsel for us -
draw near to God, and He will draw near to you.

To draw near means to have a close relationship and
fellowship. How do we draw near to God? We draw
near when we are constant in prayers. We draw near in
praise and worship of His greatness. We draw near
when we study God's Word. We draw nearer when we
take away our sins and confess them. We draw near
when we receive Jesus in Holy Communion. We draw
near when we are involved in works of mercy for the
sake of the Lord.

PRAYER

Lord Jesus, draw me nearer in love with you.
Draw my spirit close to you. May I not worship
you from afar, nor allow sin to take me to a
distant country.
Amen.

Day 24

WHOEVER SERVES ME MUST FOLLOW ME

²⁶ Whoever serves me must follow me, and where I am, there will my servant be also. Whoever serves me, the Father will honour.
John 12:26

Reflection

Jesus says whoever serves Him must follow Him. It doesn't mean that we quit our job or caring for our family or studying at school. It means we must do all those things, as a servant of Jesus. We turn our entire life and duties to the service of God. We serve God through how we live and what we do.

Jesus says where He is, there we should be. Dear Child of God, let us not be where Christ will not be. Let us not hasten to where Christ will not go. Where Jesus is, is where we ought to be.

PRAYER
Lord Jesus, may I serve you in all I do. May I be where you are at every point in time.
Amen.

BE NOT MISMATCHED WITH UNBELIEVERS

⁴ Do not be mismatched with unbelievers. For what partnership is there between righteousness and lawlessness? Or what fellowship is there between light and darkness?

2 Corinthians 6:14

Reflection

Is St. Paul telling us not to associate with unbelievers or not to make friends with people who don't practise our faith? Definitely not; even Christ associated with sinners and publicans. What St. Paul is saying here is very powerful. We should not allow ourselves to be influenced by the ways of the unbeliever. We are to be in the world but not become worldly, like a ship should be in the water but the water must not be in the ship. Dear Child of God, avoid all ungodly influence, whether through wrong associations, books, movies, music, blogs and sites, a show, magazine or program. Let us not be indiscriminate about the things we allow to influence our minds and lives.

PRAYER

Lord Jesus, as I pray that I may not be led into temptation, give me the wisdom to avoid walking in the path of temptation.
Amen.

Day 26

HUMILITY BRINGS BLESSING

⁹ He leads the humble in what is right and teaches the humble His way.

Psalm 25:9

Reflection

With humility comes great blessing. When we humble ourselves, God fills us with graces, and He fills us with knowledge and power. In every meek and humble soul, God sees the image of His Son. Many people are overly worried and concerned about the fat and cholesterol or sugar levels in their body/blood. Let us also be very concerned about pride which does great damage to a living soul.

PRAYER

Lord Jesus, give me the spirit of humility. Make me willing to learn from and imitate your example of humility.
Amen.

HIS HANDS ARE NOT TOO SHORT

See, the Lord's hand is not too short to save, nor His ear too dull to hear. Rather, your iniquities have been barriers between you and your God, and your sins have hidden His face from you so that He does not hear.
Isaiah 59:1-2

Reflection

God's people wondered why God did not seem to rescue them from their trials. They wondered if God had diminished in strength. Perhaps He lacked knowledge of their problems or interest in their plight. But this wasn't the situation. The problem with His people was their sins. Their love of sin had created a distance between them and God. Dear Child of God, this is what sin does. It creates a gap between us and God. This gap occurs even in our thinking and judgement. We no longer think alike with God. It can impede the flow of blessings. It can separate us from some of the benefits of God's love, like the prodigal son, who though still loved by the father, didn't enjoy the benefit of this love while he remained in sin. The problem is never with God.

PRAYER

Lord Jesus, give me the grace to resist sin and not allow it to come between me and God. Amen.

Day 28
COME NOW

Come now, let us argue it out, says the
Lord: though your sins are like scarlet, they
shall be like snow; though they are red like
crimson, they shall become like wool.
Isaiah 1:18

Reflection

Dear Child of God, the Lord promises to wipe and wash away our sins, no matter how weighty, dirty or gory they are. Here is a powerful promise of mercy and forgiveness. Only one thing the Lord asks of us; that is to come but not to come anytime, we must come now. No season can be better than now. Come now because you may never have another warning. Tomorrow you may not even be in this world. Today is God's time and every postponement is the devil's time. Come now that your heart is touched; tomorrow it may be hard. This is the time to come to the Lord.

PRAYER

Lord Jesus, may I hear the voice of the Spirit calling me to come now. May I never delay my opportunity for mercy.
Amen.

Day 29

CHOSEN BY THE FATHER

*² who have been chosen and destined by
God the Father and sanctified by the Spirit
to be obedient to Jesus Christ and to be
sprinkled with His blood: May grace and
peace be yours in abundance.*
1 Peter 1:2

Reflection

Dear Child of God, we have been chosen and destined by God the Father for sanctification, obedience and redemption. Sanctification means we are made holy by the power of the Holy Spirit; we are called to a life of obedience through submission to God. The blood of Jesus has been sprinkled on us as a sign of our redemption, protection and evidence that we are beneficiaries of the new covenant of grace. Let us pray that the Holy Spirit may perfect His work of holiness in God, that He may strengthen our will to be obedient and help us so to live that the blood shed for us will not be in vain.

PRAYER

Lord Jesus, thank you for what you have done to save me. May your saving work not be fruitless in my life.
Amen.

Day 30

YOUR LABOUR IS NOT IN VAIN

*⁵⁸ Therefore, my beloved, be steadfast,
immovable, always excelling in the work of
the Lord because you know that in the Lord
your labour is not in vain.*
1 Corinthians 15:58

Reflection

Because of the reality and the power of the resurrection, our labour in the Lord will never be in vain. However, let us keep in mind that it is not enough to labour, our labour must be for the Lord. That is, our labour must be under His direction and according to His instruction. The labour must be for His glory and we must persevere in the labour to the end.

PRAYER

Lord Jesus, give me the strength and joy to labour in your service, under your direction, instruction and influence and for your glory and praise alone.

Amen.

EVERY DEED SHALL BE JUDGED

14 For God will bring every deed into judgment, including every secret thing, whether good or evil.

Ecclesiastes 12:14

Reflection

It is wisdom to fear God and keep His commandments because one day, we shall all account for everything we have done, even the ones we think are secret or we think that time has healed while we refuse to repent and confess them. This is a warning for us not to live without consideration for God, for eternity, for judgement. Dear Child of God, keep in mind that you must render a full account of your life and unless your account is balanced, the gates of heaven may not open to you. This is the time we have to balance our account. It is appointed for us to die once, and after death comes judgement.

PRAYER

Lord Jesus, help me to live each moment with the consciousness that I must render an account of my entire life, not to an earthly judge but to a just judge who is all-seeing and who doesn't overlook sin.

Amen.

BOOKS BY
FR. EMMANUEL OKAMI

He Sent Forth His Word, Series 1: Homilies for Sundays, Year A.

He Sent Forth His Word, Series 2: Homilies for Sundays, Year B.

He Sent Forth His Word, Series 3: Homilies for Sundays, Year C.

He Sent Forth His Word, Series 4: Homilies for the Liturgical Seasons of Advent, Christmas, Lent and Easter.

He Sent Forth His Word, Series 5: Homilies for Feasts and Solemnities.

He Sent Forth His Word, Series 6: Homilies for Weekdays, Cycle I.

He Sent Forth His Word, Series 7: Homilies for Weekdays, Cycle II.

A Light to My Path: A Collection of Retreat Talks and Reflections.

His Voice Goes Forth: A Collection of Vocal Meditations and Nuggets.

Lord, Teach Us to Pray: Prayers for Various Occasions.

Pray Without Ceasing: Prayers for Various Occasions.

Seven Days Journey with the Lord: A Handbook for a Self-facilitated Retreat.

Praying with the Psalms.

What God has Joined Together: A Handbook for Marriage Preparation Course.

Whom Shall I Send: A Seven-day Journey with the Lord through His Word.

They Shall be Called My Children: Reflections and Prayers for Children.

When the Spirit Comes Upon You, Series 1:
A Nine-day Reflection and Prayers for the Gifts of the Holy Spirit.

When the Spirit Comes Upon You, Series 2:
A Twelve-day Reflection and Prayers for the Fruits of the Holy Spirit.

When the Spirit Comes Upon You, Series 3:
A Twelve-day Reflection and Prayers for the Manifestation of the Holy Spirit.

Become a Better Person:
A Thirty-day Journey Towards Self-improvement and Character Transformation

Vessels For Special Use:
Practical Counsels for Seminarians in Formation

In the Arms of Mary:
Thirty-One Days with Our Blessed Mother
(Fr. Emmanuel Okami and Lisa Timms)

Printed in Great Britain
by Amazon